P9-CKA-527

THE SACCO-VANZETTI CASE

On April 15, 1920, two shoe-factory employees were murdered by armed robbers in a payroll holdup in South Braintree, Massachusetts. In the search that followed, Nicola Sacco and Bartolomeo Vanzetti, aliens and anarchists, were seized as suspects. Although they were arrested by mere chance in a trap laid for someone else, Massachusetts law-enforcement officials found enough of a case against them to indict them for the crime. They were convicted on July 14, 1921. For six years, until their execution on August 23, 1927, defense attorneys fought to free the two men from what they felt was a tragic miscarriage of justice in which prejudice, fear, dishonesty, misunderstanding, bad police methods, and a rigid court system all played a part. This most controversial American trial of the twentieth century still stands as a classic demonstration of how a judicial system, if allowed to become inflexible, may lose sight of the goal of justice.

PRINCIPALS

ALESSANDRO BERARDELLI } killed in payroll holdup in South Braintree, Massa-
FREDERICK PARMENTER } chusetts, on April 15, 1920.

NICOLA SACCO } Italian anarchists convicted and executed for the
BARTOLOMEO VANZETTI } South Braintree murders.

MICHAEL E. STEWART, chief of police in Bridgewater, Massachusetts.

WEBSTER THAYER, presiding judge at trial of Sacco and Vanzetti.

FREDERICK G. KATZMANN, district attorney and prosecutor.

FRED MOORE, chief defense counsel, November, 1920-24.

JEREMIAH J. McANARNEY } assisting defense attorneys from May, 1921, to
THOMAS F. McANARNEY } December, 1924.

WILLIAM G. THOMPSON, chief counsel for the defense from November, 1924, to August 6, 1927.

HERBERT B. EHRMANN, assisting attorney for the defense from May, 1926, to August, 1927.

CAPTAIN WILLIAM G. PROCTOR, ballistics expert and prosecution witness.

CELESTINO MADEIROS (Medeiros), convicted bank robber and murderer.

ALVAN T. FULLER, governor of Massachusetts in 1927.

A. LAWRENCE LOWELL
SAMUEL W. STRATTON } members of a committee appointed by Fuller in 1927
ROBERT A. GRANT } to review the case and advise him on it.

A FOCUS BOOK

The Sacco-Vanzetti Case, 1920-27

*Commonwealth of Massachusetts vs.
Nicola Sacco and Bartolomeo Vanzetti*

by Alice Dickinson

Illustrated with maps and photographs

Franklin Watts, Inc. | New York | 1972

Title page photo: Protesting the executions of Sacco and Vanzetti, crowds fill Union Square in New York City, August 9, 1927.

Photographs courtesy:
Brown Brothers, cover, pp. 9, 20, 23, 28, 35, 74-75, 76-77
Culver Pictures, Inc., title page, pp. 6, 33, 38, 65, 67, 70
N. Y. Public Library Picture Collection, pp. 18

Library of Congress Cataloging in Publication Data

Dickinson, Alice.
    The Sacco-Vanzetti case, 1920-27.

    (A Focus book)
    SUMMARY: Outlines the events of the Sacco-Vanzetti case and debates the degree of justice done in "this most controversial American trial of the twentieth century."
    Bibliography: p.
    1. Sacco-Vanzetti case. [1. Sacco-Vanzetti case. 2. Trials (Murder)]
KF224.S2D5   345'.744'02523   72-187971
ISBN 0-531-02458-X
1P CT5991 Franklin   6170-8866   2-28   metal 4

Contents

The Bridgewater Attempted Holdup   3

First Impressions   5

Red Hysteria   8

The South Braintree Holdup   13

A Strange Trail   16

Sacco and Vanzetti   21

Vanzetti's Indictment and the Plymouth Trial   25

The Dedham Trial   32

Motions for a New Trial   55

Final Efforts   64

August 22, 1927   74

The Questions Remain   78

Chronology   82

A Selected Bibliography   84

Index   85

The authors and publisher of the Focus Books wish to acknowledge the helpful editorial suggestions of Professor Richard B. Morris.

THE SACCO-VANZETTI CASE

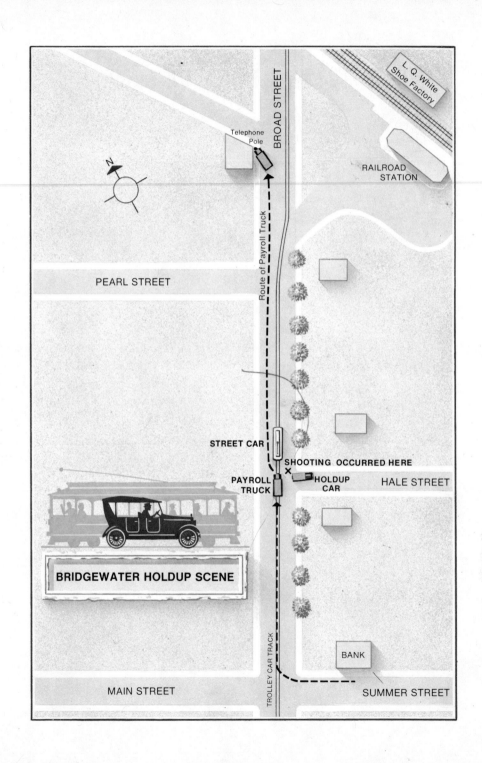

BRIDGEWATER HOLDUP SCENE

The Bridgewater Attempted Holdup

December 24, 1919, was payday at the L. Q. White Shoe Company in Bridgewater, Massachusetts. At a little after seven in the morning, the company's truck drew up at the local bank. Alfred Cox, the paymaster, carried out the payroll cash, about $33,000, and locked it in a large iron container bolted to the truck's floor. Then he climbed in and sat down on the container, his back to the driver's seat, and Earl Graves, the company chauffeur, started the car. Beside Graves sat Benjamin Bowles, a police officer armed with a revolver. The open-sided truck headed down Broad Street for the railroad tracks and the factory beyond. A short way ahead, Cox could hear the whining little trolley car that ran the length of the street to the railway station.

Just before the corner of Hale Street, branching off to the right, the trolley car seemed to slow down, then a gunshot sounded. At the same moment, Graves made a quick swerve to the left of the streetcar. Cox turned just in time to see a man with a shotgun standing about 12 feet away and aiming at the truck. Near him was another man, with a revolver. Parked at the corner of Hale and Broad streets was a big, dark, curtained touring car.

By now, the truck was disappearing behind the streetcar. The bandit shot again, and Bowles fired twice. The truck continued on its way, then skidded and came to a halt against a telegraph pole. But the trolley car had protected the payroll and the men carrying it. The bandits evidently realized that they had missed their chance. They climbed into their automobile, drove down Hale Street, and disappeared.

The whole incident was over in less than ten minutes. The holdup attempt was unsuccessful; the company truck was not seriously damaged; no one was hurt; the factory employees were paid on time.

[3]

People would talk about the affair for a few days, and that would be the end of it — or so everyone thought. Actually, this small incident was the beginning of what was to develop into the most famous American trial of the twentieth century — a trial that would awaken protests and rioting all over the world and that could still cause heated arguments fifty years later.

First Impressions

On the same day the incident occurred, the shoe company hired detectives from the Pinkerton Agency in Boston to find the guilty men and offered a reward of $1,000 for their apprehension. Early that afternoon an agency operative arrived in Bridgewater and began interviewing witnesses. Their impressions of the bandits were still clear.

The man with the shotgun turned out to be the important person in the case. Graves, the driver of the payroll truck, described him as about 5 feet 6 inches tall, about thirty-five years old, with a dark complexion and dark moustache — "He looked like a Greek." Graves spoke of the bandits' car as a "dark auto like a Hudson," and later he referred to it again as "this Hudson car."

Bowles, the guard, described the man as 5 feet 7 inches tall, weighing about 150 pounds, with a black, closely cropped moustache, red cheeks, thin face, and black hair. Bowles thought he was Italian or Portuguese.

Cox, the paymaster, described the gunman as a Russian, Pole, or Austrian, 5 feet 8 inches tall, about forty years old, and weighing about 150 pounds. The paymaster said the man had a dark complexion and a "closely cropped moustache that might have been slightly gray."

Several other persons had seen the holdup attempt. The most important of these was Frank W. Harding, an automobile salesman. He had been walking near Hale Street when he noticed a seven-passenger black Hudson touring car standing at the corner. The trolley car was coming and he saw a man step out from Hale Street as if to board it. Suddenly, this man took aim with a shotgun and fired at the payroll truck as it followed the streetcar.

[5]

Harding described the gunman as slim, about 5 feet 10 inches tall, and wearing a long black overcoat and a black derby hat. "I did not get much of a look at his face," he said, "but I think he was a Pole." Later, Harding repeated that he had not looked carefully at the man's face. He did get the license-plate number of the car: 01173C.

While the witnesses vary in some respects, they do agree that the man with the shotgun had a dark complexion, dark hair, and a dark, cropped moustache, was of medium height, and was probably of foreign origin. Graves and Harding, the chauffeur and the automobile salesman — the two witnesses most likely to know about cars — identified the automobile as a Hudson touring car.

The Pinkerton operative also interviewed Michael E. Stewart, chief of police in Bridgewater. Stewart had not witnessed the attempted holdup, but as the principal law-enforcement officer of the town he was naturally concerned. He thought the holdup was "the work of an out-of-town band of Russians with a possible confederate in the shoe factory." He told the Pinkerton man that the license plates 01173C, those on the bandits' car, had been stolen a few days earlier from a garage in Needham, a nearby town. This report turned out to be true.

Hudson touring car, similar to the one first identified in the L. Q. White Shoe Company holdup.

[7]

Red Hysteria

All four witnesses stressed the foreign origin of the bandits. Chief Stewart spoke of "out-of-town Russians." There seemed to be no basis for his theory, but in Massachusetts at that time it was perhaps a natural conclusion.

The old towns had long been proud of their fine homes and the early New England family names of their inhabitants. But the years just before World War I had brought an increase in industry and a wave of new, alien workers for the factories. Their names — Sadowski, Fruzetti, Mouradian — sounded strange to the old-timers, who were suspicious, vaguely fearful, and more than a little scornful of these "foreigners" with their European faces and their incomprehensible languages.

Now the war was over and another worry troubled many native-born Americans. In Russia there had been a Communist revolution. Many of the newcomers to America were radical in their thinking. They were anarchists, Communists, syndicalists, socialists. However harmless they might really be, they were thought of as dangerous agitators. Although no two of the radical groups thought alike, conservatives classed them all together as "Reds."

Fear of the "Reds" was nationwide. In 1919, the Attorney General of the United States, A. Mitchell Palmer, warned of radical aliens in the country who might be planning to bring about a Red revolution by violent means. Hundreds of radical periodicals had sprung up and radical clubs met regularly.

Palmer's fears seemed to be well founded when in April, 1919, dozens of bombs were mailed to judges, members of the President's cabinet, and other government bigwigs. Later, on the morning of June 3, 1919, newspaper headlines across the country screamed the

[8]

Attorney General A. Mitchell Palmer warned of radical aliens in the country.

[9]

story of midnight bombings at the homes of public officials in eight cities.

Palmer himself was one of the bombing victims. He and his family had escaped injury, but two men — either bombers or passers-by — were blown to bits. Radical literature was found near the scene, and the Justice Department decided to take steps. Plans were made to set a single night for a nationwide raid during which federal agents aided by local police would round up the radicals. Deportation proceedings could then be started against those considered dangerous.

Local raids were held for practice, and January 2, 1920, was set for the big endeavor. Agents who had joined leftist organizations managed to have meetings scheduled for that night. On January 2, in thirty-three American cities, police stormed into homes and clubs and meetings to arrest about three thousand men and women, mostly aliens, claimed to be guilty of plotting the overthrow of the United States government. Smaller raids followed. In all, they went on for nearly a year. Of the more than four thousand aliens arrested, fewer than one thousand were ever deported. Many of the foreign-born were innocent victims of the government's action.

Massachusetts shared in the mass hysteria against the "Reds." On the night of January 2, hundreds of aliens were taken to the jail on Deer Island in Boston Harbor. Many women and children were snatched from their beds, told to dress, and driven away in police patrol wagons. Rooms were searched and private possessions were seized unlawfully.

At Deer Island, although the weather was freezing, there was no heat in the crowded jail cells. Sanitary facilities were lacking. Many people were held for days before they could get in touch with friends outside. One person committed suicide and dozens more were half insane with fear. Eventually, many were released, but no foreign-born person in New England was likely to forget this time of terror.

Chief Stewart was aiding the federal officials in apprehending radicals around Bridgewater. To him, radicals were Reds and Russians. They were very much on his mind at the time of the attempted Bridgewater holdup.

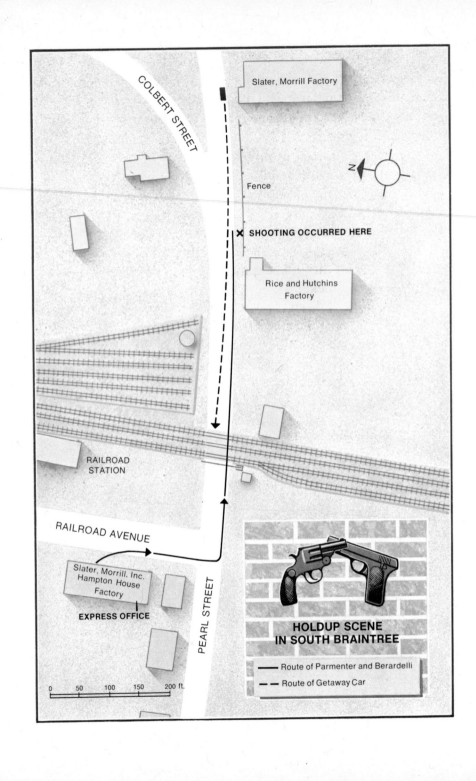

COLBERT STREET

Slater, Morrill Factory

Fence

N

X SHOOTING OCCURRED HERE

Rice and Hutchins
Factory

RAILROAD
STATION

RAILROAD AVENUE

Slater, Morrill, Inc.
Hampton House
Factory

EXPRESS OFFICE

PEARL STREET

**HOLDUP SCENE
IN SOUTH BRAINTREE**

——— Route of Parmenter and Berardelli
– – – Route of Getaway Car

0   50   100   150   200 ft.

The South Braintree Holdup

The Pinkerton men in Bridgewater learned that on November 23, 1919, a seven-passenger Buick touring car had been stolen in Needham, where the license plates had earlier disappeared. The Buick was black, with a window in its rear curtain. "This Buick may have been the car the bandits had," noted a Pinkerton man. Two well-qualified witnesses had identified the bandits' automobile as a Hudson, but from this time on, the men working on the case began to think of it as a Buick.

One clue had been found. After the shooting, Dr. J. M. Murphy, who lived on Broad Street, had picked up a gun shell and some shot near the place where the bandits had stood. The shell was for a 12-gauge Winchester Repeater.

When it became known that a reward had been offered by the shoe company, underworld informers came forward. One of them told of an Italian in Boston who said that the holdup men were Italian anarchists who had temporarily stored their car in a shack near Bridgewater. The neighborhood of Bridgewater was searched for this rumored shack, but with no success.

By April 15, 1920, no suspects had been arrested. On that day another holdup occurred — this time a successful one that resulted in two chillingly brutal murders. It, too, was directed at a shoe-factory payroll.

On the morning of April 15, in South Braintree, a town near Bridgewater, the payroll for the Slater and Morrill factory arrived on the 9:18 train from Boston. As was usual on Thursdays, the American Express agent received the locked iron box and drove with it to his office. When he had unpacked the money he took it to the Slater and Morrill office upstairs in the same building. There the paymistress put the money into pay envelopes and repacked it in two steel boxes with handles and Yale locks. By three o'clock, the payroll, almost $16,000, was ready to go to the factory, situated across the railroad track a short distance down Pearl Street.

The money was customarily carried by Frederick Parmenter and Alessandro Berardelli, who supposedly were armed. Sometimes the two men walked to the factory with the payroll and sometimes they drove. Sometimes another man went with them.

On this particular day, Parmenter and Berardelli were alone and they walked, each carrying a money box. As they passed Rice and Hutchins, another shoe factory, two men were leaning against the fence. Berardelli came opposite one of the men, who stepped forward, pulled a hand gun, and shot him. Berardelli staggered and fell, and his assailant shot him again. Parmenter ran across the street, but dropped his box when two bullets hit him in the back.

Then one of the assailants fired a shot into the air. This was evidently a signal for a dark, curtained touring car that was standing down the street in front of the Slater and Morrill factory. It came slowly up the hill as a third man stepped from behind some bricks piled at the side of the street. Two of the holdup men picked up the money boxes and all three got into the car. As it drew away, a bandit on the running board fired a final shot at Berardelli as he lay in the street, a bubble of blood frothing from his lips. A moment later, the barrel of a gun appeared at the broken-out rear window of the car. The automobile drove up Pearl Street, over the railway track, and was gone. One witness managed to get the license-plate number: 49783.

[14]

Berardelli died within a few minutes, and Parmenter lived only until the next day. Neither had been armed when he was carried from the street. An autopsy revealed four bullets in Berardelli's body, two in Parmenter's.

A Strange Trail

Pinkerton agents and the state and local police immediately began an investigation of the murders. At an inquest on April 17, two doctors and twenty-three other witnesses testified. Descriptions of the assailants varied somewhat, but it was generally agreed that the gunmen were Italian. Few of the eyewitnesses thought they could identify these men again. Several of them picked the police-file photo of Anthony Palmisano as that of one of the men. Palmisano was later found to have been in jail since January, 1920.

In all, five men had been involved in the holdup. They had used two automobiles — the dark, polished getaway car and an older, dirtier car. Both automobiles had been seen by the express agent in the morning — the drivers apparently checking to see that the payroll had arrived. The dirty car had later been observed around South Braintree by other people. Police thought the bandits might have kept it nearby to switch to with the money, so throwing pursuers off the trail.

The robbery was apparently carefully planned. The dark touring car had been stationed in front of the Slater and Morrill factory for some time before the holdup. A man kept tinkering over it, probably to make his waiting seem more plausible. The two gunmen also seemed to have been standing in a well-thought-out location.

On the same day as the inquest, Charles Fuller and Max Wind, of Brockton, were riding horseback in West Bridgewater. They turned into a little-used wood road winding off Manley Street and, after they had gone a way through the scrub oak and pine, came upon an abandoned Buick touring car with no license plates. The back window was broken out and the glass lay on the floor inside the car. The two men notified the neighboring Brockton police, who came and examined the automobile, then drove it away. It turned out to be the car stolen in Needham in November. Several South Braintree witnesses thought it might be the automobile used in the holdup and murders.

The day before the inquest, April 16, Chief Stewart of Bridge-water had received a call from the Boston Immigration Office. Feruccio Coacci, an Italian anarchist living in West Bridgewater, had earlier been arrested for deportation and had given his bond to appear in Boston on April 15, 1920. Now, with the bond expired, the immigration officer asked Stewart to check on the anarchist. The chief sent his assistant, who found Coacci ready and even eager to be deported.

Stewart remembered the informer's story to the Pinkerton agent about Italian anarchists and the Bridgewater holdup attempt, and he decided to investigate further. He found that Coacci had been living with another anarchist, Mike Boda. In back of Boda's house was a shed in which he kept his ancient Overland car. Thinking of what the informant had said about a shack and a car, Stewart was now truly intrigued. The discovery of the Buick, also in West Bridge-water, whetted his curiosity even more. But when he showed interest in Boda, the anarchist disappeared. His Overland car, however, had been left for repairs at Simon Johnson's garage in West Bridgewater. Stewart asked Johnson to notify the police when Boda called for the automobile.

On the night of May 5, 1920, at about half-past nine, the West Bridgewater police received a call from Mrs. Johnson. Boda and a friend had arrived by motorcycle and had been joined by two other men, who were walking. The four had come for the car. As there were no 1920 license plates on it, Johnson had cautioned them against taking it. The men had then left.

[17]

HARRINGTON & RICHARDSON
REVOLVERS

H. & R. Premier and "Automatic Ejecting"

The H. & R. Premier or Automatic Ejecting Model, is an efficient pocket revolver with an outside hammer and, therefore, may be shot either single or double action as desired. This model is entirely reliable, smooth working, and amply powerful for all ordinary requirements. Empty shells are automatically ejected when the revolver is opened for reloading. Nickel or blue.

.22 caliber Premier shoots .22 Short, Long and Long Rifle cartridges. The .32 caliber arm shoots the .32 S. & W. cartridge. Made with 2 or 3 inch barrel.

F104

F104. ....$14.75

The .32 caliber "Automatic Ejecting" arm shoots the .32 S. & W., .32 S. & W. Long, and .32 Colt New Police. The .38 caliber arm shoots .38 S. & W. and .38 Colt New Police. With 3¼ inch barrel.

F103. ....$14.75

Either model available with other barrel lengths:

4 inch ....$15.25   5 inch ....$15.50   6 inch $15.75

H. & R. Hammerless Revolvers

Absolutely safe, reliable and effective. To fire, you must pull the trigger. Automatic shell ejector and independent cylinder stop.

.22 Rim Fire 7 shot and .32 C. F. 5 Shot. 2 and 3 inch barrel.

F105. ....$14.75

.32 6 shot and .38 C. F. 5 shot. 3¼ inch barrel............ 14.75

Any of the above calibers in 4 inch barrel................ 15.25

Any of the above calibers in 5 inch barrel................ 15.50

F105

Any of the above calibers in 6 inch barrel................ 15.75

The H. & R. Single and Double Action Sportsman Revolver

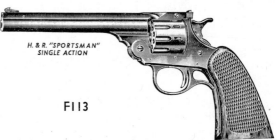

H. & R. "SPORTSMAN" SINGLE ACTION

F113

The Sportsman is a high grade, hand-fitted, super accurate revolver of most advanced design. Working parts of the action are of tool steel, hardened, tempered and hand stoned. Every one is machine rest tested for accuracy at twenty yards and must make at least half inch groups to pass inspection.

SPECIFICATIONS: Length of barrel: 3 or 6 inches. Weight with 6 inch barrel, 29 ounces. Finish: Blue with dead black top rib and sights. Number of shots: 9. Ammunition: .22 Long Rifle, either regular or high speed. Action: Single or double, hand stone, and composed of hardened tool steel parts. Trigger pull: 2½ and 3 pounds, single action; 3 to 4 pounds, double action. Exceptionally clean and sharp. Sights: 1/10 inch Patridge. Front sight adjustable for elevation, rear sight for windage.

Boda and his friend, Riccardo Orciani, had driven away on the motorcycle. The other two men had taken the streetcar for Brockton. Police arrested them on the car at about ten o'clock and took them to the Brockton station house. The two men were Nicola Sacco and Bartolomeo Vanzetti. They had no police records and apparently had never been in any kind of trouble. Yet, when they were arrested, they were both armed. Sacco had a .32-caliber Colt automatic pistol, fully loaded, and a number of extra cartridges in his pocket. Vanzetti carried a .38 Harrington and Richardson revolver, also fully loaded. In his pocket were three or four shotgun shells.

The two men were unknown to the police and had been picked up by the merest chance, in a trap really laid for Boda. If they had not been armed, it is doubtful that they would have been held for long. The loaded guns, however, marked them as suspicious characters and were reason enough for them to be detained.

Old advertisement for Harrington and Richardson revolvers. Vanzetti carried a .38 H & R revolver when arrested.

Nicola Sacco.   *Bartolomeo. Vanzetti.*

[20]

Sacco and Vanzetti

Both Sacco and Vanzetti were Italian-born. In 1908, when Sacco was seventeen, he had emigrated to the United States with an older brother. Two years later, he became a shoe-factory employee. He was married and in May, 1920, at the age of twenty-nine, had one son and was expecting another child soon.

Sacco lived and worked in Stoughton, a small town near Bridgewater. His employer, Michael Kelley of the 3K shoe factory, considered him a reliable man and a good worker. Both Sacco and his wife were active in raising money for radical causes. In 1917, he had refused to buy Liberty bonds at the factory where he then worked because he did not believe in war. In May, 1917, he had gone to Mexico with a group of pacificists to avoid military service in World War I. He returned in September, 1917, under an assumed name, and was not regularly employed until the war was over. During this time he worked for a few days at the Rice and Hutchins shoe factory in South Braintree.

Bartolomeo Vanzetti, at the age of thirteen, had left school in his native Italian village to work as an apprentice to a pastry baker. Later he moved to a bakery in a larger town and began to read widely in his spare time. In 1908, he emigrated to the United States. For eight months he worked as a dishwasher in a fashionable New York restaurant under horrendous conditions. Then he began a rambling life with a wide variety of jobs — farm laborer, chef's assistant, railway construction worker.

Eventually Vanzetti drifted to Plymouth, Massachusetts, where he was employed at the Plymouth Cordage Company. In 1916, he was active during a strike and was not rehired. In May, 1917, he went with Sacco to Mexico to avoid serving in the army. He re-entered the United States in September of that year and returned to

Plymouth in 1918. From then on, he worked fairly regularly, peddling fish from door to door.

Vanzetti was a thinker, interested in society and man's place in it. His working experiences in the United States, and his reading, had drawn him to anarchism. Through this mutual interest, he and Sacco had become friends.

Anarchists believe that compulsory government is the source of evil in society and should be done away with. In its place, they believe, voluntary self-governing groups will arise. Some anarchists think their goal can be reached only through revolution, while others think it can be reached by a process of gradual change. Their thinking is idealistic, resting on the faith that human beings, if freed from the restraints of government, will respect the rights of each individual.

In 1920, Sacco and Vanzetti and a group of fellow anarchists were collecting money for the defense of Robert Elia and Andrea Salsedo, New York Italians arrested because their shop had printed anarchist literature found near the site of one of the bombings. The Massachusetts anarchists were worried about these men and on April 25 sent Vanzetti to New York to find out what was being done about them. There, Salsedo's lawyer warned Vanzetti that further crackdowns on anarchists were likely. He advised the Massachusetts sympathizers to get rid of any radical literature they might have in their homes, to avoid possible arrest and deportation.

At their later trial, Sacco and Vanzetti gave their story of what happened thereafter. Vanzetti reported to his group on May 2 and told of the lawyer's warning. Orciani, who was at the meeting, suggested that Boda's car might be used for collecting books and pamphlets, which could be stored until danger was over. Sacco, Vanzetti, and Orciani agreed to get in touch with Boda sometime during the week.

Mrs. Sacco and child.

Salsedo had been held in a fourteenth-floor room in New York. On the morning of May 3, his lifeless body was found lying on the pavement below the window of his prison. News of his death filled the anarchist world with foreboding. Was it suicide — or murder? No one could say, but in either case it was frightening and ominous. The Massachusetts anarchists decided to collect all incriminating literature without further delay.

Sacco's mother had died some time before in Italy, and his family wished him to return with his wife and child for a visit. He had long planned the trip and was leaving within a few days. On May 5, the day of his arrest, his wife Rosina was busy packing when Vanzetti arrived. Soon Boda and Orciani came, and after supper the four men set off to get Boda's car at Simon Johnson's garage. Boda and Orciani went by motorcycle and Sacco and Vanzetti by streetcar.

Vanzetti's Indictment
and the Plymouth Trial

At the time of his arrest, Vanzetti asked the police officer why he and Sacco had been seized. "Oh, you know, you know why," the officer replied, but gave no further explanation. At no time during the long night of questioning that followed did anyone inform the men of the reason for their arrest or even hint at it. With the memory of Salsedo's fate fresh in their minds, Sacco and Vanzetti formed their own conclusions. After all, they were anarchists and draft dodgers and aliens; other men of their kind had been seized. They assumed that their turn had come and they were frightened.

Their apprehensions were only strengthened when Chief Stewart of Bridgewater arrived. He asked about their political beliefs. Were they Communists? Were they anarchists? Did they believe in the United States government?

When Stewart asked about Orciani and Boda, Sacco and Vanzetti denied knowing them. No, they replied to a question, they had not seen a motorcycle that evening. They were on their way back from Bridgewater, where they had gone to look for a friend named Pappi. They were vague, however, when asked where Pappi lived, and they did not know his last name.

The next day, District Attorney Frederick G. Katzmann queried the two men. He informed them that they did not have to answer his questions. But they did not speak English well and were uncertain of their rights.

Katzmann did not tell the men why they were being held. During his lengthy questioning he did ask if they knew of the South Braintree murders. Both Sacco and Vanzetti later claimed that they drew no inference from the questions about South Braintree and still thought they were being held because they were radicals.

[25]

Again, to Katzmann, the two men denied knowing Orciani and Boda. Vanzetti told a false story about where he had bought his revolver. Sacco said he had been working on April 15. (Katzmann was already aware that the Italian had been absent from the factory on that day.) Both prisoners gave false answers to other questions.

Stewart and Katzmann knew that Sacco and Vanzetti were lying. The two Italians acted like guilty men who were trying to conceal something. And they *had* been armed when they were arrested. In all this, Stewart saw evidence for his fast-developing theory that these men had been involved in both the Bridgewater and the South Braintree holdups.

The license plates on the car driven in the South Braintree murders had been stolen early in January, 1920, in Needham, the town from which had also come the stolen Buick car and the license plates used in the Bridgewater affair. The police saw a connection between the two holdups. It began to be taken for granted that the Buick found in West Bridgewater had been used in both affairs.

There might also be a connection, police thought, between the shotgun shells found on Vanzetti and the shell picked up by Dr. Murphy in Bridgewater.

The guns and ammunition carried by Sacco and Vanzetti were seized as possible evidence against them. But here the police were careless. They did not mark or date these objects, as they should have. Later on, when the shells were introduced as evidence in Vanzetti's Plymouth trial, there was no way of knowing whether they really were the ones that had been taken from him on May 5. They had been passed around quite casually since then, and they were bound to be slightly suspect as evidence.

Sacco and Vanzetti were fingerprinted. If their prints had matched those found on the Buick car, the two men could have been linked with the automobile. But nothing further was ever heard about fingerprints.

There had been eyewitnesses to both crimes, however, and now began a long parade of people to identify the two men in the Brockton jail. Here again, the police were at fault. In fairness to a suspect, the usual method of identification is to place him in a lineup with a group of other persons and to ask witnesses to pick out the person they saw at the scene of the crime. This procedure was not followed at Brockton. Time and again, Sacco and Vanzetti were paraded singly before witnesses, who were asked if this was the man they had seen.

Even honest witnesses find themselves becoming uncertain if they are faced several times with the same suspect and are asked to identify him positively. In this kind of situation the power of suggestion is very strong, as every lawyer knows.

In the case of Sacco and Vanzetti, the eyewitnesses did waver. Harding, who had said he did not get a good look at the face of the gunman in Bridgewater, now identified Vanzetti positively. Vanzetti, who was thirty-two, had a long, drooping, dark moustache. Cox, although he had described an older man to the Pinkerton agent at Bridgewater and had mentioned a short, cropped moustache with some gray in it, now stated that Vanzetti bore a "strong resemblance" to the man he had seen. Some of the South Braintree eyewitnesses came several times to view the suspects. One man identified Vanzetti as the driver of the getaway car. Some others stated that Sacco looked like the man they had seen.

Stewart's theory was that the holdup men were Sacco, Vanzetti, Orciani, Boda, and Coacci. No evidence could be found against Orciani, and his time-clock record showed him at work on both December 24, 1919, and April 15, 1920. Coacci had been deported. His trunk was intercepted and searched in an attempt to find the

money stolen in the South Braintree holdup. His room in West Bridgewater was gone over and some possessions he had stored with a friend were examined. No evidence was found against him. Boda had disappeared. He was a short, slight man, 5 feet 4 inches tall and weighing about 120 pounds. He would have been exceptionally noticeable to eyewitnesses. No one ever described a man resembling him in connection with either crime. Only Nicola Sacco and Bartolomeo Vanzetti remained as suspects.

On May 12, 1920, Vanzetti was charged with attempted murder and robbery at Bridgewater. His Plymouth friends persuaded him to retain a Plymouth lawyer, John P. Vahey, who was experienced in criminal cases.

At the preliminary hearing on the charge, Cox thought Vanzetti might be the gunman, but added, "The man might look different today," and later testified, "I think there is a doubt." Bowles identified Vanzetti positively, as did Harding. Graves, the chauffeur and other important eyewitness, had died since December, 1919.

On June 11, 1920, Vanzetti was indicted for assault with intent to rob and assault with intent to murder in the Bridgewater attempted holdup. His trial began at Plymouth, Massachusetts, the county seat, on June 22, 1920. The court was presided over by Judge Webster Thayer. District Attorney Katzmann conducted the prosecution's case against Vanzetti.

To prove Vanzetti guilty, the prosecution relied chiefly on eyewitness identification and circumstantial evidence. Bowles testified that Vanzetti was the holdup man and that the holdup car was a Buick. Cox identified Vanzetti as the man he had seen. On further examination, he admitted, "I can't say I am positive he is the man." Harding identified Vanzetti positively and stated that the holdup

Judge Webster Thayer presided over the courtroom at Vanzetti's Plymouth trial.

car was the Buick standing outside the courthouse — the car found in the Manley woods.

Not until many years later did Vanzetti's lawyers learn of the Pinkerton reports made immediately after the Bridgewater attempted holdup. If the defense had been aware of these interviews, it could have challenged the eyewitness evidence, especially that of Harding, who had said originally that he had not seen the gunman's face clearly, but who had definitely identified the car as a Hudson.

Other prosecution evidence was the 12-gauge shotgun shell found on the street in Bridgewater and the shells said to have been taken from Vanzetti. One of these latter was a 12-gauge Winchester Repeater shell, like that picked up by Dr. Murphy. Officer Connolly of Brockton, who had arrested and searched Vanzetti, thought the shells looked like the same ones he had found on Vanzetti. They were admitted as evidence, although there was no way of positively identifying them.

The Johnsons, Chief Stewart, and other witnesses also testified against Vanzetti.

Vanzetti's defense relied chiefly on alibi witnesses to prove that he had been in Plymouth on the morning of December 24, 1919. Eleven of these witnesses were Italians who testified that they had either bought eels from Vanzetti on that morning or had seen him delivering the fish to other people. When asked how they were sure that the day was December 24, they replied that the traditional Italian meal for Christmas Eve was eels. In anticipation of this, Vanzetti had ordered a barrel of eels from Boston. They had arrived on December 23, and he had peddled them the next day.

The most important defense witness was a thirteen-year-old boy, Beltrando Brini, who said that on December 24 he had worked all morning helping Vanzetti. His testimony and that of the other witnesses was full of little details that it would have been hard to falsify. But Katzmann led Beltrando Brini to admit that he and

Vanzetti were good friends and that the Italian adults had heard the boy rehearse his courtroom story. These circumstances did not necessarily make his testimony less true, but they probably raised doubts among the jury members.

Other witnesses testified that Vanzetti had worn a long, drooping moustache for some years — never a cropped one. Katzmann also managed to belittle this testimony.

Some of the Italian witnesses did not speak English and testified through an interpreter who was often inaccurate; others spoke English imperfectly. Undoubtedly they were handicapped in answering Katzmann's shrewd questions.

Vanzetti never took the stand in his own defense. The reasons for this are unclear. Although legally his silence should not have harmed his case, it probably did raise doubts in the minds of the jurymen. They apparently debated seriously, however, and after more than five hours returned a verdict of guilty of assault with intent to rob and guilty of assault with intent to murder.

Six weeks later, Judge Thayer sentenced Vanzetti to twelve to fifteen years for assault with intent to rob. The judge had learned that during their deliberations the jurymen had secretly opened two of the shotgun shells. This tampering with evidence in the intent-to-murder conviction could have led to a mistrial. Vanzetti's right to be tried on evidence presented in an open court had been violated. Apparently for this reason, Judge Thayer dropped the intent-to-murder part of the conviction.

The Dedham Trial

In September, 1921, with Vanzetti already a convicted criminal, Sacco and Vanzetti were charged with the murders of Alessandro Berardelli and Frederick Parmenter in the South Braintree holdup. They pleaded not guilty.

After the arrest of the two men, some of their Italian friends had formed the Sacco-Vanzetti Defense Committee to raise money for lawyers and other expenses. Members of the committee were appalled when Vanzetti was convicted of the Bridgewater attempted holdup. Neither they nor Vanzetti felt that his lawyer, Vahey, had made a good case for him. The committee members decided to seek new counsel for the defense in the South Braintree case. They asked the advice of Carlo Tresca of New York. Tresca was a well-known anarchist and the publisher of a radical weekly newspaper. His wife was active in the International Workers of the World, a leftist labor organization. She suggested Fred Moore as lawyer. Moore had done work for the I.W.W. and had a reputation for success in championing radical causes. The committee decided to retain him.

Probably no more fateful decision was made by the committee during the whole duration of the case than this one concerning Moore. No one can say how the trial might have developed under a different man, but it is just possible that a less controversial lawyer might have won a different verdict.

Moore was from California, and Massachusetts juries at that time tended to resent out-of-state lawyers. Besides that, he was a radical who made no attempt to conceal his opinions. And his style of living was flamboyant. He was a big spender who wore his hair

Carlo Tresca, well-known anarchist and publisher of a radical weekly newspaper.

long and always seemed to be surrounded by unconventional-looking people. He made no effort to tone down his habits so that they would fade into the somewhat subdued Massachusetts background.

But perhaps most serious of all was Moore's attitude toward the case. As a radical and a labor lawyer, he saw the Sacco-Vanzetti trial as another attempt by the Establishment to victimize the workingman. To raise money for the defense, he propagandized the case in such a way that it came to be regarded as a fight for radical labor. An attorney who would have seen the accused men less as a cause and more as two unfortunate individuals in a jam might perhaps have aroused more sympathy in Massachusetts.

Just before the trial began, Moore did retain two Massachusetts lawyers as associates. They were brothers — Thomas F. and Jeremiah J. McAnarney. Though not brilliant, they were competent and well regarded. They refused to enter the case until they had interviewed the accused men and their lawyer and were convinced of the innocence of Sacco and Vanzetti. Moore tended to be careless in preparing his arguments and he did not know Massachusetts ways of thinking. The advice of the McAnarney brothers might have been helpful to him if he had been willing to listen. He insisted on running the show, however, and the two lawyers entered the case so late that they had little time for preparation before the court session began.

On May 31, 1921, at Dedham, Massachusetts, the case of the Commonwealth of Massachusetts vs. Nicola Sacco and Bartolomeo Vanzetti opened for trial under Judge Webster Thayer, who had also presided at Vanzetti's Plymouth trial. The very fact that he had been judge at Plymouth should have disqualified him from a similar role at Dedham. The lawyer for the prosecution was again District Attorney Frederick G. Katzmann, who was aided by Harold P. Williams, an assistant district attorney.

[34]

Judge Thayer arriving at Supreme Court, Dedham, Massachusetts.

[35]

Five hundred persons had been summoned as prospective jurors. The first order of business was to select a jury of twelve. By Massachusetts law the judge examined each person called. The lawyers for each side could challenge the selection of as many persons as they liked for a specific cause and could challenge forty-four persons peremptorily — that is, without stating a specific cause. A peremptory challenge is used by a lawyer when, for unspecified reasons, he feels that a juror would not consider his client's case impartially.

Judge Thayer asked each prospective juror a series of questions. Among them were these: Have you expressed or formed any opinion upon the subject matter alleged in either or both of these indictments [for the murder of Berardelli and Parmenter]? Are you sensible of any bias or prejudice therein?

Almost immediately, trouble developed among the lawyers for Sacco and Vanzetti. On various occasions when prospective jurors seemed suitable to the McAnarneys, Moore rejected them. The McAnarneys felt that they were losing honest, impartial persons. Besides that, a deep antagonism was developing between Moore and Judge Thayer. Thomas F. McAnarney said later: "Whenever he [Moore] would address the court [Thayer] it was similar to waving a red flag in the face of a wolf." McAnarney may have mixed up his animals, but his meaning was clear.

The McAnarney brothers feared that there might be a definite miscarriage of justice if Moore were left in charge. In desperation they appealed to William G. Thompson, a highly respected Boston lawyer, to come into the case. The next day, Thompson listened to the proceedings at Dedham. He too noted the hostility between Thayer and Moore and even went so far as to say to the McAnarneys: "Your goose is cooked." But it was too late for him to enter the case unless Moore retired from it. Moore refused to resign.

The questioning of the five hundred prospective jurors went on through June 2. From all these, only seven jurors were chosen;

the remainder were challenged. The sheriff rounded up two hundred more candidates overnight and finally at 1:35 A.M. on June 4, the jurors, all men, were sworn in.

In the meantime, Dedham, a quiet, elm-shaded little town, was seething with excitement. Throngs of people crowded the streets. The courthouse was heavily guarded by policemen. All visitors were stopped and searched upon entering. Four times a day, in the morning and evening and at lunchtime, Sacco and Vanzetti were handcuffed together and were marched, surrounded by armed guards, from the jail to the courthouse or back again. No one could escape the impression that here were two dangerous, desperate men.

The pleading of the case finally started on June 6, 1921, with the reading of the indictment charging Nicola Sacco and Bartolomeo Vanzetti with the murder of Parmenter and Berardelli. On June 7, Assistant District Attorney Williams made his opening statement for the prosecution. Judge Thayer cautioned the jury that an opening statement is not evidence but is merely the attorney's explanation to the jury of the issues involved and his outline of the evidence that he will later offer to prove his case.

Thayer went on to say: "You must judge these cases according to the evidence which comes from the lips of witnesses who take the witness stand and who testify under oath. That is the evidence that you are to determine, and you are to determine nothing else, and you must allow nothing else to have any weight whatsoever with you."

Williams reviewed the circumstances of the killing, mentioned some of the eyewitnesses and what they claimed to have seen, and called attention to Sacco's absence from work on the day of the shooting. He spoke of the discovery of the Buick car in the woods. He then went on to Boda who, Williams claimed, had been seen driving a Buick in early April. Williams spoke of the events of the night of May 5, leading to the arrest of Sacco and Vanzetti.

[37]

Handcuffed and surrounded by guards, Sacco and Vanzetti march to the courthouse in Dedham.

[38]

The prosecution contended, Williams said, that the South Braintree crime was committed by five men; that use was made of a stolen Buick car that had been kept in the shed behind Boda's house; that on the morning of the holdup, the car was driven to South Braintree and that it picked up Vanzetti at the East Braintree railroad station, where he got off the train from Plymouth.

Williams mentioned a cap picked up at the scene of the crime and said it was similar to one worn by Sacco. He spoke of the bullets taken from the dead men and called attention to the bullet that had actually killed Berardelli, entering his back and going down through his body to his lower abdomen. It was fired from a Colt .32, and Sacco was carrying a fully loaded Colt .32 when he was arrested.

The case was one of first-degree murder, Williams said. He admitted that no eyewitness had seen Vanzetti fire a gun, but stated that evidence connected Vanzetti with the men who had committed the murders and that it placed him in the murder car.

"The law is this, gentlemen," Williams told the jury. "If two or more conspire to kill and do any joint act looking towards a killing, one is as guilty as the other."

Williams cautioned the jury: "The defendants are presumed to be innocent. . . . They do not become guilty until evidence is offered before you gentlemen to overcome that presumption of innocence." He went on to say that the prosecution must furnish strong proof of its case. Mere preponderance of the evidence was not enough in a criminal case of this kind. There must be what is called proof beyond a reasonable doubt. If the members of the jury considered the evidence against the accused men doubtful in any reasonable way the verdict must be "not guilty." It was up to the prosecution to prove the case beyond this reasonable doubt.

After the opening statement, the prosecution called eyewitnesses to the shooting and the events surrounding it. Mary Splaine, of the payroll office, testified that, hearing shots, she had looked out the window and had seen the getaway car approaching the railway track. A man was leaning out of it shooting. She identified him as Nicola Sacco.

Cross-examination by defense lawyers brought out that she had been observing the car from a second-story window at a distance of about 70 feet and that she could see the car while it traveled only about 35 feet. After the shooting she had picked the photograph of the jailed man Palmisano as that of the gunman. She had then viewed Sacco three times at the Brockton jail, always when he was alone and not in a lineup.

Moore read the testimony she had given at the preliminary hearing in Quincy on May 26, 1920. At that time she had said she was not sure Sacco was the man in the car. At Dedham, she at first denied having made such a statement but finally admitted it. She said she had changed her mind since the Quincy hearing.

One of the prosecution's important witnesses was Lola Andrews, who had gone to the Slater and Morrill factory with a Mrs. Campbell at about 11:30 A.M. on April 15, 1920, looking for work. She said that after leaving Slater and Morrill she had seen the touring car in front of the building and had asked the man tinkering with it how to get to the Rice and Hutchins factory. She identified him as Sacco.

Later the defense called Mrs. Campbell, who denied that either of the women had spoken to the man at the car. Another defense witness testified that before the trial, Mrs. Andrews had said she had not seen the faces of the holdup men. Still another defense witness stated that she had told him the "government" was "bothering the life out of her," taking her to the Brockton jail and trying to get her "to recognize those men."

John Faulkner testified that on the morning of April 15 he had been on a Plymouth train that had let Vanzetti off at East Braintree. He did not describe the railroad car correctly nor did the railroad have any record of a passenger buying a fare or presenting a ticket from Plymouth to East Braintree.

There were other eyewitnesses, but none of the eyewitness testimony was convincing.

The prosecution next pursued a line that Williams had not even mentioned in his opening statement. Using the testimony of the Johnsons, who owned the garage in West Bridgewater, the testimony of the police officers who had arrested Sacco and Vanzetti, and the testimony of the men who had questioned them at the police station, the prosecution lawyers sought to prove that the defendants showed "consciousness of guilt." Testimony stated that the arrested men had acted suspiciously and had lied about many things, presumably because they were conscious of their guilt about something they were trying to conceal — and, the prosecution claimed, that "something" was the South Braintree crime.

Next, the prosecution lawyers produced a cap found in the street after the South Braintree shooting. They contended that it was Sacco's. George Kelley, son of Sacco's former employer, testified that Sacco had sometimes worn a cap, which he hung on a nail near his workbench. Kelley refused to identify positively the cap found in the street. It had a torn lining, and the prosecution suggested that the tear was the result of the cap's being hung on the nail in the factory. Later, both Sacco and his wife denied he had ever worn a cap of this kind, with earflaps. When Sacco tried it on, the prosecution proclaimed a perfect fit. To some observers, it looked too small.

As to Vanzetti, eyewitnesses swore that he had been in the holdup car, and the prosecution sought to prove that the .38 revolver carried by him was Berardelli's and had been taken from Berardelli at the time of the murder.

James F. Bostock testified that the week before the crime Berardelli had shown him his revolver, a .38. Bostock could give no further evidence about the gun.

Mrs. Berardelli testified that her husband's revolver had looked like Vanzetti's, which was shown in court. Admittedly, she knew little about guns. She said that about three weeks before the shooting, Berardelli had taken his gun to the Iver Johnson sporting goods company in Boston to have a broken spring repaired. He had received a claim check and had given it to Parmenter, who had lent him another gun. This second revolver "looked like the first one," according to Mrs. Berardelli. She did not know whether Berardelli had ever gotten back the original gun.

Lincoln Wadsworth, of the Iver Johnson Company, had a record of receiving a .38 Harrington and Richardson revolver from Berardelli and sending it to the repair shop on March 20, 1920. It was marked as Job 94765. But the repairman had recorded Job 94765 as a .32 Harrington and Richardson that needed a new hammer, not a spring.

The Iver Johnson Company had no record of returning the revolver to Berardelli or of reselling it, yet the gun was no longer in the shop. The repairman testified in court that the hammer in Vanzetti's gun looked new. Later, defense experts denied that the hammer was new. Unfortunately, there was no record of the serial number of either Berardelli's or Vanzetti's gun, so the question of ownership could not be settled.

No eyewitness reported that the bandits took anything from Berardelli's person during the shooting and no witness could state definitely that Berardelli was carrying a revolver on April 15. The defense called witnesses who testified that Vanzetti had bought his gun.

Perhaps the most important evidence developed by the prosecution was that concerning the six bullets found in the bodies of the dead men. Five of the bullets had come from a gun that witnesses agreed was probably a .32 Savage automatic. But the sixth bullet —

the one that actually killed Berardelli — had come from a .32 Colt automatic. The prosecution sought to prove that the Colt in question was Sacco's.

Dr. George Magrath, the medical examiner who had taken the four bullets from Berardelli's body, had scratched marks on them with a needle — one vertical line for the first bullet, two vertical lines for the second bullet, and so on. The bullet marked III was the one in question.

Prosecution witnesses were Captain William H. Proctor of the Massachusetts State Police, a ballistics expert, and Captain Charles Van Amburgh, of the ballistics department of the Remington Company, gun manufacturers.

The barrel of a Colt pistol has inside rifling — a series of grooves that spiral counterclockwise. When a bullet is fired, it expands in the pistol and fills the grooves. They cause the bullet to rotate so that when it leaves the barrel, it spins and flies straight toward its target. The grooves leave marks on the bullet, and if there are flaws in the barrel, they also leave marks. The customary way to identify bullets is to observe and measure these marks. Experts for both the prosecution and the defense had fired bullets from Sacco's pistol and had compared them with bullet number III.

Captain Proctor, for the prosecution, testified that bullet number III had been fired from a .32 Colt automatic. The prosecuting attorney's questioning then went like this:

Q. Captain Proctor, have you an opinion as to whether bullet three was fired from the Colt automatic which is in evidence [Sacco's pistol]?

A. I have.

Q. And what is your opinion?

A. My opinion is that it is consistent with being fired by that pistol.

[43]

This answer was somewhat less than straightforward; it did not state that the bullet unquestionably had come from Sacco's gun. But the lawyers for the defense failed to challenge Proctor's testimony.

When Captain Van Amburgh was asked the same question about the bullet, he was not much more positive: "I am inclined to believe that it was fired, number three bullet was fired, from this Colt automatic pistol [Sacco's]."

Van Amburgh then went on to demonstrate the bullet markings and spoke of pitting in the gun barrel that would leave a particular mark on the bullet. When questioned by the defense lawyers about the pitting, Van Amburgh replied, "I believe it was caused by rust."

The defense lawyer went on: "When you say 'I believe,' have you anything back of that that you don't feel sure of?"

Van Amburgh answered, "Yes, I have a slight reservation."

Later, the defense introduced its experts, James E. Burns, a ballistics engineer for the U.S. Cartridge Company, and J. H. Fitzgerald, of the Colt firearms factory in Hartford, Connecticut. Both men testified that in their judgment, bullet number III had not been fired from Sacco's gun.

The ballistics evidence was highly technical and was probably puzzling to the jury, which had only the help of a low-powered magnifying glass in observing the bullet markings.

As to the Buick car found in the Manley woods, no prosecution witness was able to identify it positively as the getaway car. When the automobile was shown to the jury at Dedham, it had a bullet hole in its right-hand side. Yet neither of the men who had found the car on April 17, 1920, had noticed such a hole, nor had the policemen who had inspected the car before taking it to Brockton. Since that time, the automobile had been passed around among the Brockton police, the state police, and garage employees. Moore noted that there had been many opportunities for making changes in the car and moved that the jury should be instructed to disregard all evidence concerning it. Judge Thayer denied the motion, saying that it is the jury's province to decide if the evidence should be considered seriously.

The prosecution did not succeed in showing any connection between the Buick car and Boda's shed, as it had intended. Accordingly, the judge instructed the jury to disregard all testimony about the shed.

After nineteen days, the prosecution completed its case against Sacco and Vanzetti and it was the defense's turn.

Of the seventeen eyewitnesses for the defense, two had noticed the murder car before the shooting. They swore that they had not seen either of the defendants in the automobile. Thirteen eyewitnesses had observed the holdup. They testified that Sacco was not one of the men who had taken part in it. Prosecutor Katzmann was able to discredit some of the witnesses in cross-examination. Two eyewitnesses were unable to state an opinion as to the identity of the murderers.

After testimony about Vanzetti's revolver and bullet number III, the defense called Bartolomeo Vanzetti to the witness stand.

In calling Vanzetti, and later Sacco, to testify, the defense lawyers faced a serious dilemma. So far in the trial, the question of the defendants' radicalism had not been raised. Now it was bound to enter the case. Although the prosecution had made no such accusation, Chief Stewart's theory was that Boda and his companions had wanted the Overland on the night of May 5, 1920, so that they could hold up another payroll the next day. Once the prosecution started asking about the car, the defendants would have to explain why they had called for it at Johnson's garage.

There was another matter, too. The prosecution had noted the lies told by Sacco and Vanzetti when they were arrested and had claimed "consciousness of guilt," indicating that the two men were trying to conceal their part in the South Braintree murders. Sacco and Vanzetti's reasons both for lying and for trying to get the car would reveal that they were anarchists. Their lawyers were well aware that in Massachusetts at that time, when Italians were commonly referred to as "wops" or "dagos" or "guineas," any courtroom evidence that these men were also deeply committed "Reds" might hopelessly prejudice their case with the jury. Yet the lawyers had no choice. Sacco and Vanzetti had to take the witness stand if they were to have any chance at all of going free.

Vanzetti was questioned by his lawyer, Jeremiah J. McAnarney, about his activities on April 15, 1920, the day of the South Braintree murders. On this question, too, both the defendants ran into difficulties. Sacco had not been working and so lacked the alibi of a time-clock record. Vanzetti led a freewheeling life and it was difficult for him to prove just where he had been on any given day in the past. He claimed to have been in Plymouth on April 15, to have bought a piece of cloth from a peddler, and to have talked with various people around the town.

Later, the people he mentioned were called to the witness stand. Most of them had trouble in pinpointing April 15 as the day they had talked with Vanzetti.

McAnarney questioned Vanzetti concerning his whereabouts just before May 5, 1920, and Vanzetti told of his trip to New York and of going to West Bridgewater with Boda, Sacco, and Orciani. He spoke of their plan to collect the radical literature from their friends and testified about his arrest.

When asked why he was armed, Vanzetti said, "It was a bad time and I like to have a revolver for self-defense." He stated that he often carried a good deal of money when he went to Boston to buy fish for his business. As to the shells in his pocket, he said Mrs. Sacco had given them to him on May 5, when she was packing.

MAIN ROADS
+--+--+ RAILROADS

0   5   10   15   20
Miles

**ROUTES FROM BOSTON
TO PLYMOUTH**

Boston
DEER IS.
*Boston
Harbor*

● Needham
Dedham ●
Quincy ●
Braintree ●
E. Braintree
So. Braintree

*MASSACHUSETTS

BAY*

Stoughton ●
Hanover ●
Brockton ●
W. Bridgewater ●
Bridgewater ●
Plymouth ●

M A S S A C H U S E T T S

N

New Bedford ●

R.I.

*Buzzards
Bay*

They had been left by friends who had been shooting in the woods behind the house. Vanzetti said he took the shells for one of his Plymouth acquaintances who went bird hunting.

Vanzetti explained his lies to the police by saying he had been sure the arrest was because of his draft-dodging and his radicalism. Frightened, he had wanted to conceal everything about his activities and about his anarchist friends, whom he had wished to protect from arrest and deportation.

In cross-examination, Katzmann stressed the fact that Vanzetti was a draft dodger. Vanzetti freely admitted going to Mexico in 1917 to escape military service. On the whole, he acquitted himself well as a witness.

Now Nicola Sacco took the stand. The questions asked him covered some of the same ground as in Vanzetti's testimony, and the answers confirmed what Vanzetti had said.

When asked where he was on April 15, 1920, Sacco replied that he had gone to the Italian consulate in Boston to get a passport for his trip to Italy. He had left Stoughton in the morning. In Boston, he had met a friend by chance and had visited some clothing stores. After that, it was lunchtime and Sacco had gone to Boni's, an Italian restaurant. There he had seen more friends and had eaten with them. He had then gone to the Italian consulate. But instead of bringing passport-sized pictures of his family, he had brought a large photograph, which could not be accepted. As a result, no passport record was made; he was told to come back another time with proper photographs. He had drunk coffee with friends, had bought some groceries, and had taken a late afternoon train to Stoughton.

The men he had seen in Boston testified for him. The prosecution questioned exactly what day Sacco had been in the city. Two of the men fixed the date by explaining that, at lunch and later over coffee, there had been discussion of a banquet to be given by Italian newspapermen for the editor of the *Boston Evening Transcript*. Sacco's two friends had been invited to the affair, and they remembered that it took place on the same day they discussed it with Sacco. The passport official who had interviewed Sacco had gone back to Italy, but he claimed to remember the incident of the photograph, and the date. His sworn testimony was read into the court records.

Further confirmation of Sacco's trip came from an unexpected source. One day during the trial, Sacco, who had a good memory for faces, saw in the courtroom a man who looked familiar. Sacco finally placed him. This man had sat across the aisle on the train from Boston on April 15 and had also gotten off at Stoughton. Sacco told one of the McAnarneys, who questioned the man, James Hayes.

Hayes was a highway engineer who, having business at the Dedham courthouse, had dropped in at the trial by chance. Upon returning home and consulting his records, he found that April 15, 1920, had indeed been the date of a trip he had taken to Boston. He did not know Sacco, nor had he noticed Sacco on the train. He was willing to testify, however, as to where he had sat, and in which car, on the train. Sacco did not hear the testimony, but on being recalled to the courtroom, he gave his own account of the train ride. He and Hayes agreed on details. The prosecution never challenged the testimony.

As to his being armed when arrested, Sacco explained that on the afternoon of May 5, he and Vanzetti had planned to shoot in the woods, to use up the bullets he had, before he left for Italy. Sacco had put his revolver in his belt and the bullets in his pocket, but Boda and Orciani had arrived and his plans had changed. He said he had forgotten to put aside his revolver when he started for West Bridgewater.

The truly damaging part of Sacco's testimony came when he was questioned about his political beliefs. In reply to a question, he had told of coming to the United States. "My brother . . . he desired to come to this country, so I was crazy to come . . . because I was liked a free country." Katzmann used this statement to lead Sacco into a long speech on his political beliefs.

Q. [by Katzmann]. Did you say yesterday you love a free country?
A. Yes, sir.

Katzmann quickly interpreted Sacco's general love of a free country as love for the United States.

Q. Did you love this country in the month of May, 1917? [This was the time when Sacco went to Mexico to escape military service.]
A. If you can, Mr. Katzmann, if you give me that, — I could explain —

With Sacco begging for a chance to explain and with the defense attorneys shouting their objections, Katzmann persisted.

Q. There are two words you can use, Mr. Sacco, yes or no.
A. Yes.

Katzmann went on to draw from Sacco a confused statement of his reasons for love of the United States. The reasons were material — money, food — and Sacco tried in vain to suggest there were other things in love for a free country.

[50]

When Jeremiah McAnarney again objected to the discussion, Judge Thayer answered: "I think you opened it [this whole line of questioning] up."

"No, your Honor, I have not," McAnarney answered.

"Is not your claim," Judge Thayer asked, "that the defendant, as a reason that he has given for going to the Johnson house, that they wanted the automobile to prevent people from being deported and to get this literature all out of the way? Does he not claim that that was done in the interest of the United States, to prevent violation of the law by the distribution of this literature?"

McAnarney claimed no such thing as "interest of the United States," and it is difficult to believe that Judge Thayer thought he did. After a long wrangle, during which the judge kept repeating his question, McAnarney finally said: "If your Honor please, the remarks made with reference to the country and whether the acts that he was doing were for the benefit of the country. I can see no other inference to be drawn from these except prejudicial to the defendants."

Judge Thayer then cautioned the jury to ignore the whole conversation between him and McAnarney. But he had joined the prosecution in its argument, and his antagonistic attitude toward the defense had become all too apparent. How much effect this would have on the jury remained to be seen.

Katzmann proceeded with his questioning of Sacco.

Q. What did you mean when you said yesterday you loved a free country?

Sacco was a man passionately devoted to his cause, and here was a chance to explain his feelings.

[51]

A. . . . When I came to this country I saw there was not what I was thinking before, but there was all the difference, because I been working in Italy not so hard as I been work in this country. I could live free there just as well. . . . When I been started work here very hard and been work thirteen years, hard worker, I could not been afford much a family the way I did have the idea before. . . . I could no push my boy some to go to school and other things. . . . The free idea gives any man a chance to profess his own idea . . . to give a chance to print and education, literature, free speech. . . . I could see the best men, intelligent, education, they been arrested and sent to prison and died in prison for years and years without getting them out, and Debs, one of the great men in his country, he is in prison, still away in prison, because he is a socialist. He wanted the laboring class to have better conditions and better living, more education . . . but they put him in prison. Why? Because the capitalist class . . . they don't want our child to go to high school or to college. . . . They want the working class to be a low all the times, be underfoot, and not to be up with the head. . . . So that is why my idea has been changed. So that is why I love people who labor and work and see better conditions every day develop, makes no more war. . . . That is why I love socialists. That is why I like people who want education and living, building, who is good."

And so it went, with Katzmann leading Sacco on and forcing him to admit that he had gained many advantages by living in the United States, even though he criticized it and had refused to fight for it. Meanwhile, the defense lawyers were objecting to this line of questioning, which was far from the central issue of the trial. A judge has the power to stop a lawyer's questioning if it does not relate to the defendant's crime and is objected to by the opposing attorney. But Judge Thayer made no such move and repeatedly overruled the defense attorneys' objections.

Sacco's words fell strangely in the courtroom. It was only a short time since the end of World War I, during which patriotism had burned at fever pitch. It was an even shorter time since Attorney General Palmer's raids and their conjuring up of Red bogeymen. How would the jury react? Lawyers for the defense were worried.

At last, on July 13, 1921, the lawyers' final arguments began. Each side was allowed four hours to present its condensation of the trial's testimony. Katzmann had the advantage of speaking last. He was in a position to attack the rather inept performances of Moore and Jeremiah McAnarney. Katzmann's summing up was powerful and skillfully adapted to his purposes. It could well have impressed the jury.

When the lawyers had finished, Judge Thayer gave his charge to the jury, explaining the law in relation to the evidence. He made several mistakes in stating testimony, which he corrected when the defense called them to his attention. He persisted in referring to the defendants as "slackers" — a loaded word in Massachusetts at that time. And he opened his remarks by comparing the jury to "true soldiers" who had responded to the call for their services "in the spirit of supreme American loyalty."

"For he who is loyal to God, to country, to his state, and to his fellowmen, represents the highest and noblest type of true American citizenship," he said. These words may have served as a reminder to the jury that the men they were judging had shown no such loyalty.

Judge Thayer again cautioned the jury that any finding of "guilty" must have been proven beyond a reasonable doubt. He outlined the main points of the trial: (1) identification of the defendants by eyewitnesses; (2) statements concerning bullet number III, which killed Berardelli; (3) statements concerning Vanzetti's revolver and the possibility that it had belonged to Berardelli; (4) the cap found at the scene of the crime and claimed to be Sacco's; (5) consciousness of guilt — did the defendants lie out of fear because of their political beliefs or in order to hide their part in the crime at South Braintree? and (6) the alibis of the defendants.

It is notable that Thayer, in his charge to the jury, took Proctor's testimony to mean that bullet number III had definitely come from Sacco's pistol.

At 2:30 P.M. on July 14, 1921, the members of the jury retired to consider their verdict. In an incredibly short time, by 7:30 P.M. that same day, they had reached their decision. In the hush of the courtroom, the foreman gave the verdict and the other jurors agreed. It was the same for both defendants: "Guilty of murder in the first degree."

As the judge adjourned the court, Sacco's shout broke the stillness: "They kill an innocent man. They kill two innocent men."

Motions for a New Trial

In Massachusetts at that time, the penalty for murder in the first degree was death in the electric chair. But before the convicted men were sentenced, the defense lawyers made several motions, or applications, for a new trial. One additional motion was made after sentencing. These motions were filed and were decided on by the court over a period of six years, during which Sacco and Vanzetti remained in prison.

The first motion contended that the jury's verdict had been against the weight of the evidence. According to Massachusetts law at that time, motions were heard by the trial judge. Judge Thayer denied the motion in December, 1921, saying that he could not set aside the verdict unless it could be shown that the jurors' judgment was badly mistaken or that they had acted in bad faith, and he felt he could not go against their opinion.

The seven motions that followed called attention to newly discovered evidence that, in the opinion of the defense, deserved careful scrutiny in a new trial.

On November 8, 1921, the Ripley motion was filed. Fred Ripley had been the foreman of the jury. During the trial he had carried in his pocket three .38-caliber cartridges like those in Vanzetti's revolver. He had shown them to other jurors and had used them for comparison with the Vanzetti cartridges. Ripley had died since the trial, but two of the jurors stated they had seen the cartridges.

On October 1, 1923, a supplement was added to this motion. It was an affidavit signed by William Daly, an old friend of Ripley's. Daly stated that in 1921 he met Ripley, who was on his way to Dedham to answer the jury summons. Daly had remarked that he did not think Sacco and Vanzetti were guilty. Thereupon, Daly claimed, Ripley replied: "Damn them, they ought to hang them anyway."

If Ripley did discuss his cartridges with the jury, he used evidence not introduced in court — a violation of due process of law. And if Ripley made the statement that Daly swore to, he was badly prejudiced and should not have served as a juror in the case. The pre-trial examination of jury candidates had included a question about prejudice.

Judge Thayer denied the Ripley motion, but in so doing, he did not refer to the Daly affidavit.

The Gould motion was filed on May 4, 1922. Roy Gould had been walking behind Parmenter and Berardelli an April 15, 1920. As the holdup car passed him, after the shooting, the man next to the driver fired a bullet through Gould's coat. Gould had given evidence to the police at the time, and the prosecution knew of him but had not called him as a witness. Now he swore that neither Sacco nor Vanzetti was in the car.

Judge Thayer denied the Gould motion, saying that it was merely one more piece of eyewitness testimony. He stated that the verdicts against the defendants had not rested on eyewitness testimony, but on consciousness of guilt.

The next two motions for a new trial attacked the means by which the prosecution had obtained testimony from two of its witnesses, Carlos Goodridge and Lola Andrews. These motions were also denied by Judge Thayer.

The Hamilton-Proctor motion, filed in two separate parts during 1923, had to do with the guns and bullets used in the murders. The evidence of the firearms experts at the trial had been careless and confusing. The defense now offered the opinion of another expert, Albert H. Hamilton. He denied that bullet number III had come from Sacco's gun. Two prosecution experts gave contrary opinions.

The other part of this motion concerned Captain William H. Proctor, who in 1921 had been one of the prosecution's expert witnesses at the trial. In 1923, Proctor signed an extraordinary affidavit for the defense. He stated that during the preparation for the trial the prosecution lawyers had repeatedly asked him if he could justify the opinion that bullet number III had come from the pistol carried by Sacco. He had made all possible tests, he said, but was not able to find any evidence to support this opinion. He had so informed the district attorney and his assistant before the trial.

At the trial, Proctor had said, "My opinion is that it [the bullet] is consistent with being fired by that pistol."

In his 1923 affidavit, Proctor stated: "That is still my opinion, for the reason that bullet number III, in my judgment, passed through some Colt automatic pistol, but I do not intend by that answer to imply that I found any evidence that the so-called mortal bullet had passed through this particular Colt automatic pistol [Sacco's] and the district attorney well knew that I did not so intend, and framed his question accordingly. Had I been asked the direct question, whether I had found any affirmative evidence whatever that this so-called mortal bullet had passed through this particular Sacco's pistol, I should have answered, as I do now, in the negative."

In replying to Proctor's affidavit, neither District Attorney Katzmann nor his assistant disputed what Proctor's true opinion had been. They only denied that they had *repeatedly* asked him about the bullet or that he had *repeatedly* answered. The assistant district attorney also stated that Proctor himself had suggested the questions to be asked him in court.

Shortly after he filed his affidavit, Proctor died, so Judge Thayer did not have an opportunity to question him. On October 1, 1924, the judge denied the Hamilton-Proctor motion. He cleared the prosecution attorneys of any attempt to frame questions so that

Proctor could answer in a way misleading to the jury. Proctor, said the judge, had been free to give his honest opinion in court. He must have meant exactly what he said and the jury must have completely understood his meaning. Accordingly, his testimony was not prejudicial to the defendants. But Judge Thayer himself, in his charge to the jury at the end of the trial, appears to have understood Proctor to mean that the bullet had come from Sacco's gun.

Sacco and his wife and the Sacco-Vanzetti Defense Committee had become more and more dissatisfied with Moore's handling of the case. On November 8, 1924, the Defense Committee succeeded in getting him to resign, although he stepped down unwillingly. On November 25, 1924, William G. Thompson became general counsel for the defense. He had been the McAnarneys' choice to replace Moore back in 1921.

Attorney Thompson was a man deeply committed to his profession. Although nothing could have been further from his own philosophy than anarchism, he was convinced that Sacco and Vanzetti were innocent and had been unjustly treated. As a matter of conscience, he was willing to fight for them.

Starting in the fall of 1924, four defense motions for a new trial already denied by Judge Thayer were appealed to the Supreme Judicial Court, the highest court in Massachusetts. On May 12, 1926, the court gave its decision: "Exceptions overruled. Verdict to stand."

Under Massachusetts law at that time, the Supreme Judicial Court — the court of appeal — could review the records and procedures of a case to make sure that they met the legal standards for a fair trial. The court of appeal could not, however, weigh the evidence anew.

There was an important factor in the Sacco-Vanzetti case — the discretionary powers of the judge. A judge's duty is to sit impartially, using his "discretion" in making decisions on questions that come up daily in the trial — among them, what should be admitted as evidence. The defense attorneys held that Judge Thayer had used his discretionary powers in a way that worked against the defendants. After considering the trial record and hearing the attorneys' arguments, the Supreme Judicial Court decided that Judge Thayer had conducted the trial properly, that many matters had rightly rested on his discretion, and that he had not misused it.

While the appeal to the Supreme Judicial Court was still being considered, new evidence came to light. A small-time criminal, Celestino Madeiros (also spelled Medeiros), had committed murder during a bank holdup and was being held in the Dedham jail awaiting the outcome of an appeal of his conviction. He knew that Sacco was also in the jail and had tried to get in touch with him. Sacco had ignored him because state and federal spies intent on detecting radical activities had been placed near his cell at various times and he was suspicious. But finally, on November 18, 1925, a jail runner delivered a note to Sacco that read as follows:

I hear by confess to being in the south Braintree shoe company crime and Sacco and Vanzetti was not in said crime. [Signed] Celestino F. Madeiros

Sacco gave the note to Attorney Thompson, who immediately talked with Madeiros. The bank robber claimed he was confessing because he felt sorry for Rosina Sacco and her children, whom he often saw visiting the jail. The story Madeiros told was this:

Some Italian men he knew in Providence, Rhode Island, had for a long time been stealing shipments of shoes and other merchandise from freight cars and claimed to have taken part in many holdups. A few days before April 15, 1920, they asked Madeiros to come along on the South Braintree job, which they were then planning.

There had been four men in the holdup besides Madeiros, he said. He had sat on the back seat holding a Colt .38. The car curtains were drawn and flapping and he had not seen much of the action. Two cars had been involved — a Buick, used in South Braintree, and a Hudson, into which the men had changed afterward in a patch of woods in nearby Randolph. Madeiros refused to tell the names of the holdup men, but he said enough so that an investigation could be started.

When the Massachusetts law authorities refused to cooperate, Thompson sent his young assistant, Herbert B. Ehrmann, to Providence to look for more evidence. Ehrmann took on the assignment with hope, but with some doubt.

Before long, he was pursuing the case with increasing excitement. There was an Italian gang, the Morelli brothers, well-known in Providence for their criminal activities. They were out of jail on April 15, 1920; they were in need of money to pay for an impending trial on another crime; some of them answered the descriptions given by eyewitnesses of the South Braintree holdup; the photograph of one of them bore a striking resemblance to Nicola Sacco. They had stolen many shoe shipments from Slater and Morrill in South Braintree and were familiar with the factory and its procedures. Their guns were like those described by the firearms experts at the trial.

The more Ehrmann worked on the case, the more unexplained things fell into place. Of the five men who committed the crime, only Sacco and Vanzetti had ever been apprehended as suspects. Madeiros' story accounted for all the holdup gang. Ehrmann followed the trail to New Bedford, where he learned that before Sacco and Vanzetti were arrested, the New Bedford police had actually suspected the Morellis. Investigation of them had been dropped when the two anarchists were seized.

Meanwhile, James Weeks, Madeiros' accomplice in the bank robbery for which he was imprisoned, had told Thompson that he had known Madeiros for several years and that Madeiros had often spoken of the South Braintree holdup. Weeks confirmed that it was arranged by a gang made up chiefly of the Italian Morelli brothers of Providence.

Ehrmann collected evidence from many sources — enough to persuade him and Thompson that here, at last, was the big break in the case. A motion for a new trial on the basis of the Madeiros evidence was presented to Judge Thayer on May 26, 1926. Along with it, another motion outlined evidence that Katzmann had worked a deal with the Department of Justice for its help in securing a conviction of Sacco and Vanzetti or at least in gaining enough evidence of their radicalism so that they could be deported. For the department's help, Katzmann was said to have promised to try getting from the two men any information that might lead to the deportation of other radicals.

Judge Thayer heard arguments on the motions, and on October 23, 1926, handed down his decision denying them. Of Madeiros, he stated that the man was a crook, a liar, and a person who had been convicted of murder and that he, the judge, could not "find as a fact that Madeiros told the truth."

Madeiros' story did show some weaknesses, but the defense lawyers felt it was important enough to be heard by a new jury at a new trial.

Parts of the public who had previously viewed the Sacco-Vanzetti case as a matter of routine justice were also swinging to that opinion. On October 26, 1926, three days after Judge Thayer's denial, the conservative *Boston Herald* published an editorial that read, in part:

In our opinion Nicola Sacco and Bartolomeo Vanzetti ought not to be executed on the warrant of the verdict returned by a jury on July 14, 1921. We do not know whether these men are guilty or not. . . . But as months have merged into years and the great debate over this case has continued, our doubts have solidified slowly into convictions, and reluctantly we have found ourselves compelled to reverse our original judgment. We hope the Supreme Judicial Court will grant a new trial on the basis of the new evidence not yet examined in open court. . . .

We have read the full decision in which Judge Webster Thayer, who presided at the original trial, renders his decision against the application for a new trial, and we submit that it carries the tone of the advocate rather than the arbitrator. . . .

Now, as to Madeiros . . . he may be lying, but the criterion here is not what a judge may think about it but what a jury might think about it. The question is — Would the new evidence be a real factor with a jury in reaching a decision?

We submit that doubt is cast on the verdict of the jury by the important affidavit made after the trial by Captain W. H. Proctor of the state police. . . . His affidavit states what the record implies, that a device was fixed up in advance for dodging a direct answer to a direct question. His replies were understood to mean that he believed the bullet came from that weapon. He allowed that impression to go abroad. But his affidavit contradicts that testimony. . . .

If on a new trial the defendants shall again be found guilty, we shall be infinitely better off than if we proceed to execution on the basis of the trial already held.

Attorney Thompson appealed the denial of the Madeiros motion to the Massachusetts Supreme Judicial Court on January 27, 1927. In March, public opinion was aroused even more when Felix Frankfurter, a professor at the Harvard Law School and later a distinguished Supreme Court Justice, published an article in the *Atlantic Monthly*, detailing the many injustices to the defendants during the case. The *Atlantic Monthly*, highly respectable and highly revered, was by no means a radical magazine. Its publication of such. a piece, by such an author, served to sway more minds to the cause of Sacco and Vanzetti. Opinion was further inflamed when, on April 5, the Supreme Judicial Court upheld Judge Thayer.

Every possible legal means of getting a new trial seemed now to have been exhausted. On April 9, 1927, the district attorney asked that the two men be sentenced.

"Nicola Sacco," asked the clerk, when the court had assembled, "have you anything to say why sentence of death should not be passed upon you?"

Sacco rose to state his innocence and to assert again his faith in the cause of the common man.

Vanzetti, in turn, claimed innocence and protested the oppression of man. He spoke of the hostility of Judge Thayer and went on to an eloquent final plea:

"This is what I say: I would not wish to a dog or to a snake, to the most low and misfortunate creature of the earth — I would not wish to any of them what I have had to suffer for things I am not guilty of. But my conviction is that I have suffered for things that I am guilty of. I am suffering because I am a radical, and indeed I am a radical. I have suffered because I was an Italian, and indeed I am an Italian. I have suffered more for my family and for my beloved than for myself, but I am so convinced to be right that if you could execute me two times, and if I could be reborn two other times, I would live again to do what I have done already.

" I have finished. Thank you."

The moment of sentencing had come. The men were to die in the electric chair sometime during the week beginning on July 10, 1927.

For one final time, Sacco's cry rang through the courtroom: "You know I am innocent. That is the same words I pronounced seven years ago. You condemn two innocent men."

[63]

Final Efforts

More and more, public opinion around the world was opposing the execution of the two Italians. The defense lawyers succeeded in having the week of execution changed to August 10 so that they might have more time to fight the sentence.

On May 3, a petition for clemency was presented to Massachusetts Governor Alvan T. Fuller. It was signed only by Vanzetti and had been written mainly by him. Sacco, convinced that nothing now could save him and his friend, refused to sign. But Vanzetti still had a faint hope. "We are beaten, yes," he said, "but not yet lost — we may still win."

In his petition, Vanzetti did not ask for a pardon, but for a thorough review of the case. He asserted that the trial had been unfair and the judge prejudiced. He blamed the verdict of "guilty" on the feeling against radicals.

Upon receiving the petition, Governor Fuller immediately began his own investigation. He was a successful businessman, not a lawyer, yet he hoped to decide the guilt or innocence of Sacco and Vanzetti. In vain, Attorney Thompson pointed out how difficult it is for an inexperienced person to weigh testimony. He begged Fuller to consider only if the trial had been fair.

The governor allowed no defense lawyers in the room while he questioned witnesses, and no record of the proceedings was made public. Again in vain, Thompson warned that witnesses might say anything they chose if they were not challenged.

Fuller's secretary, Herman MacDonald, was hostile to the defense, and several disheartening incidents occurred. The defense attorneys learned of the governor's opinion that if Vanzetti was guilty of the Bridgewater attempted robbery, he was probably guilty of the South Braintree affair as well. By now, the defense knew of the

Massachusetts Governor Alvan T. Fuller began his own investigation of the Sacco-Vanzetti case.

Pinkerton reports made after the Bridgewater attempt. They were strong evidence of Vanzetti's innocence. Thompson and Ehrmann sent a résumé of the reports to Fuller, but later Fuller seemed to be unacquainted with it.

Fuller also had remarked that no evidence was ever shown that a shipment of eels had been sent to Vanzetti just before Christmas in 1919. Yet Vanzetti's alibi at Plymouth was based on his peddling the eels. Upon hearing of Fuller's comment, Ehrmann and a member of the defense committee headed for the Boston fish piers. They visited every Italian fish stall until finally they found a dealer who remembered Vanzetti as a customer. A search of his records revealed nothing, but suddenly he thought of a box of old American Express receipts in the attic. And there it was! In an old receipt book, under the date of December 20, 1919, a Saturday, was a record of eels shipped to "B. Vanzetti, Plymouth, Massachusetts." The eels would·have arrived on December 23, just as witnesses at the trial had said. Jubilant, the two men sent the receipt book to Governor Fuller. There was no response.

One day, an agitated young man came to Thompson. He was Beltrando Brini, who as a boy had helped Vanzetti deliver the eels and had testified at the Plymouth trial. Brini *knew* that Vanzetti was in Plymouth all that day, he said, and he was positive that Vanzetti was innocent of the South Braintree murders. He had spoken to Governor Fuller, but had not been given time to tell his story fully. He begged Thompson to help him see Fuller again. The attempt was made, but Fuller's secretary, MacDonald, refused an appointment. Young Brini was forced to talk to MacDonald, instead. It was doubtful if his story would go further, Thompson and Ehrmann realized.

On June 1, 1927, Governor Fuller appointed a committee to review the trial record, to interview the people who had figured in the case, and to advise him. There were three committee members:

A. Lawrence Lowell, president of Harvard University, was a member of the committee appointed by Governor Fuller to advise him on the case.

[67]

Samuel W. Stratton, president of the Massachusetts Institute of Technology; Robert A. Grant, a former judge of the probate court; and A. Lawrence Lowell, president of Harvard University. Many Massachusetts citizens breathed a sigh of relief, especially at Lowell's appointment. Here, at last, it was thought, was a man who would view the case impartially.

Lowell, however, was not a particularly good choice for the committee, nor were the other two men. Lowell was a Boston blue-blood with little grasp of criminal law or of the social and political factors involved in the case. Stratton and Grant also lacked a broad viewpoint and a knowledge of criminal law.

On July 11, 1927, the committee began questioning witnesses. Counsel for the defense was allowed to cross-examine all of them except the eleven surviving jurors, Judge Thayer, and the chief justice of the Supreme Judicial Court. The defense lawyers hoped to convince the committee that the trial evidence combined with the evidence in the succeeding motions was enough to raise reasonable doubt of the guilt of the condemned men — doubt that might at least justify a new trial. The lawyers also hoped to show that Judge Thayer's hostility to the accused was such that he was unfit to have been in charge of the case.

Some new evidence was uncovered during the hearings. South Braintree Chief of Police Gallivan testified that it was he who had made the tear in the cap, used by the prosecution to identify it as Sacco's. Gallivan had been trying to find a name tag in the lining. He also stated to the committee that the cap was not found in the street until a full day after the murders.

Proctor was said to have claimed the innocence of Sacco and Vanzetti strongly in private.

Lincoln Wadsworth of the Iver Johnson Company, who had testified for the prosecution at the trial, now stated that "there were thousands of times more chances" that Vanzetti's revolver had not been the one owned by Berardelli than that it had been. He had previously worked for the Justice Department and said that at the time of the trial he had been prejudiced against "Reds." He spoke of the "atmosphere of prejudice" at the trial and said he was now testifying before the committee as a matter of conscience.

Some new evidence concerned bullet number III. At the time of the trial, ballistics methods were crude and unreliable. By 1927, there had been developed a comparison microscope that made greater accuracy possible. In June, 1927, a ballistics expert examined bullet number III with the microscope and stated that the bullet had been fired from Sacco's pistol. Defense attorneys, however, on examining the bullet, claimed that the vertical lines labeling it as III had been made with a heavier and blunter instrument than that used to number the other bullets. All these bullets had been handled carelessly as pieces of evidence, and now the defense raised the question whether the original bullet number III might have been replaced by a substitute.

In another piece of important evidence, witnesses of undoubtedly good reputation testified that during the course of the trial they had heard Judge Thayer, outside the courtroom, speak of Sacco and Vanzetti and their lawyers in terms that were bigoted, sneering, and extremely vindictive. Thayer seemed to be almost obsessed in his hatred of "Reds," it was stated. Other witnesses described the judge's attitude toward the defendants in the courtroom as scornful and prejudiced. The actual records of the courtroom trial showed no personal remarks that were blatantly prejudiced, however.

"Would sneers show?" asked Attorney Thompson.

On July 27, the committee submitted its report to Governor Fuller. It attempted to answer three questions: Was the trial fairly conducted? Was the newly discovered evidence such that a new trial ought to have been granted? Should Sacco and Vanzetti be considered guilty of murder beyond a reasonable doubt?

Armed guards outside the prison where Sacco and Vanzetti were held.

[70]

On the first question, the committee concluded that the trial had been fair. Katzmann's long cross-examination of Sacco about his political views was said to have been justified. The committee had questioned the jurors about the courtroom atmosphere. The jurors claimed they had not been influenced by it, nor had they considered Judge Thayer anything but scrupulously fair.

As to Judge Thayer's conduct outside the courtroom, the committee concluded that he had been indiscreet: "He ought not to have talked about the case off the bench, and doing so was a grave breach of official decorum." The committee went on to say, however, that it did not believe that he used some of the expressions attributed to him and that it thought the witnesses had exaggerated. Furthermore, it did not think that what the judge said outside the courtroom affected his conduct at the trial or the opinions of the jury.

On the question of new evidence, the committee did not feel it was of sufficient weight to warrant another trial.

On the question of guilt, the committee stated its belief that Sacco and Vanzetti were guilty beyond a reasonable doubt. Concerning bullet number III, they dismissed the defense's doubts about its genuineness, saying that no credible evidence had been offered to prove it was a substitution.

The records of evidence heard by the committee do not bear out its findings. The three members seem to have believed only the evidence they wanted to believe. They apparently were more anxious to uphold the procedures of the Massachusetts courts than to judge the case impartially. The issue had become an emotional one, in which the preservation of the established order seemed all-important.

On August 3, Governor Fuller issued a statement, the result of his own conclusions and those of the committee.

"I believe with the jury, that these men, Sacco and Vanzetti,

[71]

were guilty, and that they had a fair trial. I furthermore believe that there was no justifiable reason for giving them a new trial."

There now seemed little hope for the accused men, but on August 6, the defense lawyers filed a motion for a new trial, stating that the judge was so prejudiced against the defendants and their lawyers that they did not have a fair trial. As it was customary procedure in Massachusetts for the trial judge to hear motions, Judge Thayer was about to rule on Judge Thayer's prejudice. Defense attorneys asked that another judge be allowed to hear the motion. The request was refused. Judge Thayer denied prejudice and ruled that according to Massachusetts law no motion for a new trial could now be granted because sentence on the accused had already been passed and the trial had ended. The defense attorneys appealed the ruling to the Massachusetts Supreme Judicial Court.

Early in the evening of August 10–11, Sacco and Vanzetti were made ready for electrocution. Thirty-six minutes before they were to die, Governor Fuller postponed their execution until midnight of August 22, in order to await the decision on the defense appeal. On August 19, the Supreme Judicial Court upheld Judge Thayer's ruling that it was now too late to have a new trial. Nothing more could be done for the accused within the judicial system of Massachusetts.

Early in August, the defense lawyers had attempted to transfer the case to a federal court, but that court held that the circumstances did not give it the authority to interfere with the proceedings of a state court.

Two days before the execution date, the defense lawyers asked the United States Supreme Court to review the conviction of Sacco and Vanzetti. The request was refused, on the ground that the higher court had no authority to meddle with the case of a crime charged under state law and tried by a state court.

Every possible legal means to help Sacco and Vanzetti had now been exhausted. As August 22 approached, worldwide protests against the execution became stronger. A feeling of uneasiness grew. On August 19, the *New York World* took note of this feeling in a long editorial asking for a new trial, or at least a stay of execution. It read, in part:

> The Sacco-Vanzetti case is clouded and obscure. It is full of doubt. The fairness of the trial raises doubt. The evidence raises doubt. The inadequate review of the evidence raises doubt. The governor's inquiry has not appeased these doubts. The report of his advisory committee has not settled these doubts. Everywhere there is doubt so deep, so pervasive, so unsettling, that it cannot be denied and it cannot be ignored. No man, we submit, should be put to death where so much doubt exists.

August 22, 1927

On the evening of August 22, attorneys Ehrmann and Thompson visited Governor Fuller to request a stay of execution. It was refused.

Around the world there was turmoil. In European and South American countries, mobs rioted and marched on United States embassies to stone them. In France and Italy as well as in the United States, many workers struck in protest against the execution of Sacco and Vanzetti.

As the hour of death drew near, several thousand people

gathered outside the roped-off area around the Charlestown jail where the two men were held. Beyond the throng, hundreds of cars wound themselves into a giant traffic jam. The jail itself was manned by five hundred policemen in addition to the usual prison guards. They were armed with machine guns, gas and tear bombs, and hand weapons.

When it was Sacco's time to die, just after midnight, he walked steadily to the death chamber. "Long live anarchy," he shouted in Italian, and spoke a farewell to his wife and children and friends.

Protesting the executions of Sacco and Vanzetti in Paris, France.

As Vanzetti entered the death chamber he shook hands with the warden. "I want to thank you for everything you have done for me, warden," he said. Again he protested his innocence, and just before his death, said, "I wish to forgive some people for what they are doing to me."

Warden Hendry of the jail was overcome with emotion. Never before had a condemned man thanked him. More than that, he had grown to like and respect Vanzetti.

Policemen and citizens outside the Charlestown, Massachusetts, jail, waiting for news of the executions.

The Questions Remain

Over forty years have passed since the execution of Sacco and Vanzetti, but many questions persist.

Were the two men guilty? Possibly no one will ever now be certain. Over the years, new reports have come to light. Fred Moore, the defense lawyer originally in the case, claimed to have investigated further after his dismissal and to have concluded that Sacco was guilty, Vanzetti probably innocent. How much Moore's bitter feelings about the case entered into his judgment, no one knows.

Carlo Tresca, the anarchist who had supported the two Italians, told a friend in 1943 that Sacco was guilty, Vanzetti innocent. By chance, he was interrupted before he could explain, and his political assassination some days later prevented further discussion. Some supporters of Sacco and Vanzetti claim that Tresca was merely echoing Moore's opinion. On the evidence presented at both the Plymouth and the Dedham trials, Vanzetti would certainly seem to have been innocent.

In 1961, ballistics experts using the most modern methods again compared bullet number III with bullets shot through Sacco's pistol. Their conclusion was that the fatal bullet had come from Sacco's gun. Sympathizers with Sacco and Vanzetti remember the careless handling of evidence and question, Is bullet number III the original bullet, or was there a substitution at some point?

Other reports have been heard since the execution. Supporters of Sacco and Vanzetti view these reports in one way, detractors view them in another. Those people who believe in Sacco's guilt do not accuse him of robbery and murder for personal gain, but claim he was so much of a fanatic about anarchism that he would have robbed for the cause. In the vain search for the stolen money, how-

[78]

ever, no anarchist group was found to have suddenly acquired any large sum after the holdup.

But, putting aside the matter of guilt or innocence, there are important questions having to do with law and justice.

If, at the time of their arrest, Sacco and Vanzetti had obtained a lawyer before they talked to the police, would he have discovered the true reason for their arrest? Knowing definitely that they had been arrested under suspicion of the South Braintree murders and not for their radical activities, would the two men still have lied? If they had not lied, would they have been accused of the murders? How much did their radicalism have to do with their being accused, tried, and convicted? Was there an attempt to railroad them because they were anarchists?

Would more scientific police methods after the arrest have resulted in different testimony at the trials?

Was the trial fair? Did the judge show prejudice? Did the jury show prejudice, conscious or unconscious? Reliable witnesses claimed that in various ways Judge Thayer showed his hostility to the defense. A reading of the trial record shows an obvious attempt by the judge to stay within the limits of a fair trial, and he did caution the jury at various times on the importance of impartiality. Yet, particularly during Katzmann's questioning of Sacco, in Thayer's charge to the jury, in many decisions relying on his discretion during the trial, and in his denial of some of the motions for a new trial, the judge himself was less than impartial. His conduct outside the courtroom revealed a violent bias against the defendants and their lawyers. As a hater of "Reds," the judge seems to have been a partisan of the prosecution.

Members of the jury, questioned years later, claimed their complete lack of prejudice. Several of them stated that it was the

[79]

evidence concerning bullet number III that convinced them of the two men's guilt.

No one today can wholly judge on the question of prejudice. The trial record reveals only words spoken, not tone or emphasis, not dark looks or sniffs of disdain. It was a time when public feeling was highly inflamed against radicals and aliens. The atmosphere in the police-guarded Dedham courtroom was hostile to the defendants, and the day-after-day testimony of the many witnesses was bound to dull the sensibilities of listeners. Under these conditions, is it not possible that even a well-intentioned juror might perhaps unconsciously have given way to prejudice?

In his attempt to obtain a conviction against the accused, District Attorney Katzmann suppressed evidence favorable to the defense, tried to prejudice the jury in his questioning of Sacco, consented to a framing of Proctor's testimony that was prejudicial to the defendants, and generally pursued his case beyond the limits of professional ethics. Should he have done this? Various court decisions have stated that a district attorney's obligation is not so much to win a case as to see that justice is done.

Should Sacco and Vanzetti have had another trial? There were eight motions for a new trial, seven of them based on new evidence. At the time, each motion was considered separately, and some of the motions were not significant enough to warrant further action. But the accumulated evidence in all of them certainly was serious enough to have been considered by a new jury.

Was there reasonable doubt of the defendants' guilt? Much of the evidence presented against them at the trial was weak and of little value, and some evidence in their favor seems not to have been given the careful consideration it deserved. Even the ballistics evidence, which seemed decisive to the jury, was presented in a partisan way — one team of paid experts testifying for each side. There were certainly enough grounds for doubt so that a new trial or a stay of execution should have been ordered.

Does the strict observance of law and of proper judicial procedures necessarily lead to justice? In the Massachusetts of the 1920's the answer was no. Although the evidence presented in the Sacco-Vanzetti case cried out for judicial review, a higher court of appeal in Massachusetts could judge only on the issues of law, not of fact. Moreover, the trial judge himself was the one who considered new motions. At every point in the Sacco-Vanzetti case, the defense attorneys came up against Judge Thayer. As time went on, he became more interested in self-justification than in justice.

Massachusetts lawyers themselves recognized the possibility of injustice in the state's system. In 1927, they recommended that a legislative act be passed giving the Supreme Judicial Court more power in capital cases. Finally, in 1939, Massachusetts court procedures were changed so that the higher court could review a whole case, evidence and all; could hear motions for a new trial; and could order a new trial if the court was satisfied that "the verdict was against the law or the weight of the evidence, or because of newly discovered evidence, or for any other reason that justice may require."

Should there be a death penalty? In a case like that of Sacco and Vanzetti, where there is a public atmosphere that leads to prejudice and where doubts arise, a sentence of life imprisonment would make possible a future review of the case. Would not that serve the ends of justice better?

These are some of the questions that remain and that have kept the Sacco-Vanzetti case alive and controversial. With the questions, the arguments persist. They serve a good purpose if they help awaken Americans to the importance of continually scrutinizing the courts and the law and of endlessly asking, "Is justice being done?"

CHRONOLOGY

December 24, 1919: Bridgewater attempted holdup.

January 2, 1920: Nationwide sweep to round up "Reds," with a view to deporting dangerous agitators.

April 15, 1920: South Braintree holdup and murders.

May 5, 1920: Sacco and Vanzetti arrested.

June 11, 1920: Vanzetti indicted for Bridgewater holdup.

June 22–July 1, 1920: Trial of Vanzetti at Plymouth.

August 16, 1920: Vanzetti sentenced for assault with intent to rob in Bridgewater attempted holdup.

September 11, 1920: Sacco and Vanzetti indicted for South Braintree murders.

May 31, 1921: Trial of Sacco and Vanzetti begins at Dedham.

July 14, 1921: Jury finds Sacco and Vanzetti guilty of murder in the first degree.

November 5, 1921: Motion for new trial filed as against the weight of the evidence.

November 8, 1921: Ripley motion filed.

December 24, 1921: Motion for new trial as against weight of evidence denied.

May 4, 1922: Gould motion filed.

July 22, 1922: Goodridge motion filed.

September 11, 1922: Andrews motion filed.

April 30, 1923: Hamilton section of Hamilton-Proctor motion filed.

October 1, 1923: Daly supplement added to Ripley motion.

November 5, 1923: Proctor section of Hamilton-Proctor motion filed.

October 1, 1924: Judge Thayer denies all motions.

Fall, 1924–Fall, 1925: Motions appealed to Supreme Judicial Court.

November 18, 1925: Celestino Madeiros sends confession note to Sacco.

May 12, 1926: Supreme Judicial Court denies motions and upholds convictions of Sacco and Vanzetti.

May 26, 1926: Madeiros motion presented to Judge Thayer.

October 23, 1926: Madeiros motion denied.

January 27, 1927: Denial of Madeiros motion appealed to Supreme Judicial Court.

April 5, 1927: Supreme Judicial Court upholds Judge Thayer on Madeiros motion.

April 9, 1927: Sacco and Vanzetti sentenced to death.

May 3, 1927: Petition for clemency sent to governor.

June 1, 1927: Governor appoints advisory committee to review case.

August 3, 1927: Governor Fuller upholds jury verdict and judge's sentence.

August 6, 1927: Motion for new trial on grounds of judge's prejudice.

August 8, 1927: Judge Thayer denies motion.

August 19, 1927: Supreme Judicial Court upholds Judge Thayer's ruling on motion.

August 23, 1927: Sacco and Vanzetti executed.

A SELECTED BIBLIOGRAPHY

Ehrmann, Herbert B. *The Untried Case: The Sacco-Vanzetti Case and the Morelli Gang.* New York: The Vanguard Press, 1933.

———. *The Case That Will Not Die: Commonwealth vs. Sacco and Vanzetti.* Boston: Little, Brown and Company, 1969.

Fraenkel, Osmund K. *The Sacco-Vanzetti Case.* American Trials Series, edited by Samuel Klaus. New York: Alfred A. Knopf, 1931.

Frankfurter, Felix. *The Case of Sacco and Vanzetti: A Critical Analysis for Lawyers and Laymen.* Boston: Little, Brown and Company, 1927.

Joughin, Louis, and Morgan, Edmund M. *The Legacy of Sacco and Vanzetti.* Introduction by Arthur M. Schlesinger. Chicago: Quadrangle Books, 1964.

Russell, Francis. *Tragedy at Dedham: The Story of the Sacco-Vanzetti Case.* New York: McGraw-Hill Book Company, 1962.

The Sacco-Vanzetti Case: Transcript of the Record of the Trial of Nicola Sacco and Bartolomeo Vanzetti in the Courts of Massachusetts and Subsequent Proceedings, 1920–1927. 2nd ed. Prefatory essay by William O. Douglas. 5 vols. Supplemental volume including Bridgewater Trial, Mamaroneck, N.Y.: P. P. Appel, 1969.

Weeks, Robert P., ed. *Commonwealth vs. Sacco and Vanzetti.* Englewood Cliffs, N.J.: Prentice-Hall, Inc., 1958.

INDEX

Anarchists, 8, 13, 18, 22-24, 25, 32, 48, 58, 75, 78-79
   see also: Radicals; "Reds"
Andrews, Lola, 40, 56
Appeal, motions for, 55-63
Atlantic Monthly, 62-63

Berardelli, Alessandro, 14-15, 32, 36, 37, 39, 41-43, 53, 54, 56, 69
Berardelli, Mrs. Alessandro, 42
Boda, Mike, 18-19, 22, 24, 25-27, 29, 37, 39, 45, 46, 49
Bombings (1919), 8-10, 22
   see also Palmer, A. Mitchell, raids of
Boni's (Italian restaurant), 48
Bostock, James F., 41
Boston Herald, 61-62
Bowles, Benjamin, 3, 5, 29
Bridgewater, Mass., attempted holdup at, 3-4, 5, 11, 26, 27, 29
   see also: Pinkerton agents; Plymouth trial; Stewart, Michael E.
Brini, Beltrando, 30-31, 66
Burns, James E., 44

Campbell, Mrs. (witness), 40
Coacci, Feruccio, 18, 27-29
Colt firearms factory (Hartford, Conn.), 44
Communists, 8, 25
   see also: Radicals; "Reds"
Conolly, Officer (Brocton, Mass.), 30
Cox, Alfred, 3, 5, 27, 29

Daly, William, 55-56

Death penalty, assessment of, 81
Debs, Eugene V., 52
Dedham trial, 32-54
   assessment of, 79-81
   motions for new trial following, 55-63, 80-81
   Sacco's testimony at, 48-53, 71, 79
   Vanzetti's testimony at, 45-48
Deer Island (Boston), jail on, 10
Defense Committee (Sacco-Vanzetti), 32, 58, 66
Department of Justice, 61, 69

Ehrmann, Herbert B., 60-61, 66, 74
Elia, Robert, 22

Faulkner, John, 40-41
Fitzgerald, J. H., 44
Frankfurter, Felix, 62-63
Fuller, Governor Alvan T., 64-73 passim, 74
Fuller, Charles, 16-18

Gallivan, Police Chief (South Braintree), 68
Goodridge, Carlos, 56
Gould, Roy, 56
Grant, Robert A., 68
Graves, Earl, 3, 5, 7, 29

Hamilton, Albert H., 56-58
Hamilton, Proctor motion, 56-58
Harding, Frank W., 5-7, 27, 29-30
Hayes, James, 49

Hendry, Warden (Charlestown jail), 76-77

International Workers of the World (I.W.W.), 32
Iver Johnson Company, 42, 68

Johnson, Simon, 18, 24, 30, 41, 45, 51
Justice Department, 61, 69

Katzmann, Frederick G., 25-26, 29, 30-31, 34, 45, 48, 50-52, 53, 57, 61, 71, 79, 80
Kelley, George, 41
Kelley, Michael, 21, 41

Lowell, A. Lawrence, 68
L. Q. White Shoe Company, 3, 5, 13

MacDonald, Herman, 64, 66
McAnarney, Jeremiah J., 34, 36, 46, 49, 51, 53, 58
McAnarney, Thomas F., 34, 36, 49, 58

Madeiros, Celestino, 59-62
Magrath, Dr. George, 43
Massachusetts court procedures, 81
    see also: Supreme Judicial Court; Thayer, Judge Webster
Medeiros, Celestino. See Madeiros
Mexico, Sacco and Vanzetti in, 21, 48, 50
    see also World War I
Moore, Fred, 32, 36, 40, 44-45, 53, 58, 78
Morelli brothers (Providence), 60-61

Murphy, Dr. J. M., 13, 26, 30

New York World, 73

Orciani, Riccardo, 19, 22, 24, 25-27, 46, 49

Palmer, A. Mitchell, 8-10
    raids of, 10, 53
Palmisano, Anthony, 16, 40
Parmenter, Frederick, 14-15, 32, 36, 37, 42, 56
Pinkerton agents: and Bridgewater holdup attempt, 5-7, 13, 18, 27, 30, 66
    and South Braintree murders, 16
Plymouth Cordage Company, 21, 41
Plymouth trial (of Vanzetti), 26, 29-31, 34, 66, 78
Proctor, Captain William H., 43-44, 54, 62, 68, 80
    motion for new trial of, 56-58

Radicals, 8, 25, 32, 34, 45, 61, 64, 79, 80
    See also: Anarchists; "Reds"
"Reds," 8-11, 46, 53, 69, 79
    see also: Anarchists; Radicals
Remington Company (gun manufacturers), 43
Rice and Hutchins shoe factory, 14, 21, 40
Ripley, Fred, 55-56
Russians, 8
    see also "Reds"

Sacco, Nicola: arrest of, 19, 25-27

background of, 21-24
defense attorneys for, 32-34, 36, 44 (*see also:* McAnarneys; Moore; Thompson)
efforts to save, 57-73
execution of, 74-75
and petition for clemency, 64-72
sentencing of, 63
testimony of (Dedham trial), 48-53, 71, 79
see also Dedham trial
Sacco, Mrs. Rosina, 24, 48, 58, 59
Sacco-Vanzetti Defense Committee, 32, 58, 66
Salsedo, Andrea, 22-24, 25
Slater and Morrill shoe factory, 13-15, 16, 40, 60
Socialists, 8, 52
see also: Radicals; "Reds"
South Braintree, Mass., holdup and murders at, 13-15, 16, 25-27 passim
Madeiros' confession to, 59-62
see also Dedham trial
Splaine, Mary, 39-40
Stewart, Michael E. (Police Chief), 7, 8, 11, 18, 25-26, 45
Stratton, Samuel W., 68
Supreme Judicial Court (Mass.), appeals to, 58-59, 62, 63, 68, 72, 81
Syndicalists, 8
see also: Radicals; "Reds"

Thayer, Judge Webster, 29, 31, 34, 36, 37, 45, 51, 68, 69
assessment of, 79, 81
charge to jury of, 53-54, 79
and motions for new trial, 55-63
passim, 72
Thompson, William G., 36, 58
and Governor Fuller, 64-72 passim, 74
and Madeiros' confession, 59-62
3K shoe factory, 21
Tresca, Carlo, 32, 78

U.S. Cartridge Company, 44
U.S. Supreme Court, appeal to, 72

Vahey, John P., 29, 32
Van Amburgh, Captain Charles, 43-44
Vanzetti, Bartolomeo: arrest of, 19, 25-27
background of, 21-24
and Bridgewater holdup attempt, 29 (*see also* Plymouth trial)
defense attorneys for, 32-34, 36, 44 (*see also:* McAnarneys; Moore; Thompson; Vahey)
efforts to save, 55-73
execution of, 74, 76-77
and petition for clemency, 64-72
Plymouth trial of, 26, 29-31, 34, 66, 78
sentencing of, 63
testimony of (Dedham trial), 45-48
see also Dedham trial

Wadsworth, Lincoln, 42, 68-69
Weeks, James, 60-61
Williams, Harold P., 34, 37-39, 41
Wind, Max, 16-18
World War I, Sacco and Vanzetti during, 21, 48, 50, 52, 53

ABOUT THE AUTHOR

The Sacco-Vanzetti case has long been of interest to Alice Dickinson, who grew up in Bridgewater, Massachusetts, where the affair had its beginning.

Now a resident of New York City, Miss Dickinson has been a teacher and a librarian and is now an editor in a New York publishing house. She is the author of a number of books for children, including *The Boston Massacre, The Stamp Act* (both Focus Books), *Charles Darwin and Natural Selection,* and *The First Book of Prehistoric Animals.*